VISION IN THE DESERT

Other Karl Momen books:
Homage to William Shakespeare and Richard Wagner
The Odyssey of an Artist

VISION IN THE DESERT

THE TREE OF UTAH
– A SCULPTURE BY MOMEN

HERMAN DU TOIT

PUBLISHED BY AGREKA BOOKS, SALT LAKE CITY, UTAH, USA

Published by Agreka™ Books, www.utahbooks.com
Scandinavian distributor: Silander & Fromholtz Förlags AB.
sf@stockholm.mail.telia.com

Designed by Christian Wirsén, c.wirsen@swipnet.se
Coordination Carl-Gustav Yrwing
Cover photography by Clint Helton©, heltonc@inconnect.com
Photography by Bagrat Kuprashvili, François Camoin, C. Harris, David Hawkinson, Clint Helton, George Janecek, Tim Kelly, Don Reimann, ©individual photographers
Map design by Larry Clarkson, © Clarkson Creative, Salt Lake City, Utah

ISBN 1888106891
Library of Congress 00-100328

Printed in Sweden by Wallin & Dalholm Boktryckeri AB, Lund. 2000

Agreka Books

Salt Lake City, Utah.

Contents

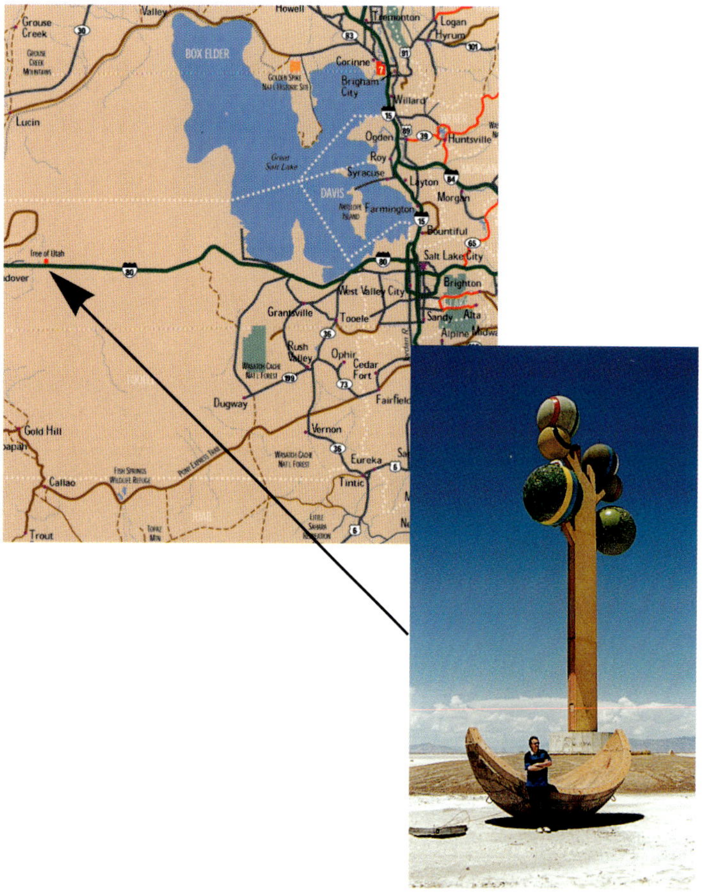
Grouse Creek
Valley
Howell
Tremonton
Logan
Hyrum
BOX ELDER
Corinne
Golden Spike Nat'l Historic Site
Brigham City
Willard
Lucin
Ogden
Huntsville
Great Salt Lake
Roy
Syracuse
Layton
DAVIS
Morgan
Farmington
Bountiful
Tree of Utah
Salt Lake City
Brighton
West Valley City
Grantsville
Tooele
Sandy
Alta
Rush Valley
Ophir
Cedar Fort
Dugway
Fairfield
Gold Hill
Vernon
Eureka
Callao
Fish Springs Wildlife Refuge
Tintic
Trout

Preface

At Milepost 26, near Wendover, Utah, Karl Momen's art installation, "The Tree of Utah," stands as a monument to one man's devotion to his art. The metaphor created and installed by Karl Momen is a gift from the artist to the desert and to all those who observe this piece as they approach the stark, but beautiful, Great Basin. We see, as the artist surely did, the visually compelling desert which on first view seems empty, but further observation reflects and enhances every element of the ecosystem. The Tree and its contrast to the environment may seem jarring to the observer, yet it wears well, becoming like the desert itself, always changing yet always remaining the same.

Bonnie H. Stephens
Director Utah Arts Council

The Utah Arts Council mission: Believing that the arts are essential to a high quality of life, the Utah Arts Council serves all the people of Utah. In response to the legislative mandate of 1899 "to advance the arts in all their phases," the Utah Arts Council broadens the availability and increases the appreciation of the arts by distributing funds, providing training and development, and providing educational programs in the arts statewide.

The Utah Arts Council lends support to Karl Momen and his generous gift to the people of the State of Utah. Proceeds from the sale of this book will be donated to the Utah State Division of Facilities Construction and Management for deposit into a fund designated for the conservation and maintenance of the Tree of Utah.

Acknowledgments

Even the slightest endeavor, no matter how inconsequential, is always achieved with the supporting influence of others. In writing and compiling this book I would like to thank Don Reimann who endured lengthy interviews, and who supplied valuable information about the technical construction of the Tree and its components. Khosrow Semnani graciously provided additional information and access to documents in his possession. I am indebted to Bonnie Stephens, Director, and Carol Nixon, former Director of the Utah Arts Council for their insightful observations and encouragement in this project. I am grateful to Clint Helton of Salt Lake City for his stunning cover photography, and Christian Wirsén, the designer of the book, for working with me through multiple modifications to the text. Thanks are also due to Anna Greta Leijon, former Swedish Minister of Labor, for permission to use excerpts from her autobiography, and to Björn Anzén for his Swedish translation. My special thanks go to Carl-Gustav Yrwing who coordinated the project. Finally, and most significantly, I would like to thank Karl Momen who was always generous with his time and with help with my questions, and who made the Tree of Utah a reality.

Introduction

The story of the Tree of Utah is one of the most remarkable in the history of public sculpture in the State of Utah. It is remarkable because of the way in which anomalous events, unrelated people, and unique environmental conditions conspired to produce one of this State's most remarkable and controversial public sculptures. At the center of this confluence of human and geographical factors stands the Tree's creator, Karl Momen, a Swedish national of Persian descent who orchestrated the entire project. The Tree has been lauded as a unique manifestation of one man's artistic intent. It was through the single-minded determination and resourcefulness of this unlikely visitor that the people of this western state became the unwitting heirs to such a significant manifestation of the modernist tradition. Momen had always adopted a highly idiosyncratic approach to his art and it was through this desire to follow a highly individualistic path that he arrived at a result that became entirely his own. The Tree has become recognized as a unique, if somewhat controversial, addition to Utah's cultural and topographical environment.

The construction of the Tree brought together an unlikely alignment of people of divergent but complementary predispositions. Utah has a reputation for being one of the most politically and culturally conservative states in the Union. Yet the people of this western state maintain well-established international connections through the history of their pioneer heritage. They are generally very friendly and accepting of foreigners in their midst. This region was originally settled by an influx of people drawn from several European countries, as a result of the early proselytizing efforts of the Church of Jesus Christ of Latter-day Saints, which is headquartered in Salt Lake City. The large missionary program of this dominant religious community continually sends and returns many of its members to all parts of the world, resulting in a local community that not only has strong familial and social links with foreign communities, but which is increasingly well informed about international cultures. It came as an unexpected but perhaps fitting tribute to the cosmopolitan connections of the people of this region that a chance visit by a Swedish artist, who happened to be passing through Salt Lake City, resulted in the conceptualization of one of Utah's most intriguing art works, executed at great personal expense to its creator. The Tree is also a tribute to several local personalities who contributed magnanimously, in various ways, to its successful completion, often in the face of overwhelming obstacles.

The unique environment of the Great Western Desert contributed an important element to the conceptualization of the Tree in the mind of Karl Momen. The Tree was criticized by environmentalists at the time of its January 1986 dedication as an unwelcome and insensitive intrusion upon the pristine expanse of desert, 26 miles east of the Nevada border. However, a counter argument from another interest group held that the Tree relies on the foil created by the bland desert landscape to achieve its particular formalist aesthetic, and that it enhances the essential features of the land. In this respect the symbiotic relationship between the desert, the Tree, and its sculptor was perhaps best expressed by a visitor to the dedication ceremony who commented: "God made the background and Momen the foreground."

The Great Basin on which the Tree is located has had an interesting history that sets it apart from most other geographical areas on the planet. In prehistoric times this area known as the Great Basin was covered by a vast expanse of water, about 19,000 square miles in area, known to geologists as Lake Bonneville. As the precipitation decreased, the lake gradually grew smaller, resulting in the Great Salt Lake, which has become one of the saltiest bodies of water in the world and the largest inland sea of salt water in the Western Hemisphere. The shoreline of the prehistoric Lake Bonneville can still be traced on the mountainsides. The receding waters left broad beaches or terraces, creating the Bonneville Salt Flats, site of the fastest automobile raceway in the world. It was here that Gary Gablich drove his rocket powered car, Blue Flame, to a speed of more than 620 miles per hour. Standing on the Flats one can see the curvature of the earth. It has been said that the Great Western Desert is a place of extreme speed, extreme heat, extreme cold, and extreme boredom. Interstate 80 stretches west for 120 miles from Salt Lake City to the Nevada border at Wendover; the last 50 mile segment of this road is arrow-straight and unremittingly monotonous to motorists. It was in this region that Nancy Holt worked from 1973 to 1976 on a 40 acre parcel of desert, framing the Great Basin landscape, in circles, with her Sun Tunnels. Her husband, the late Robert Smithson (1938 - 1973) created the Spiral Jetty (1970) near Promontory Point. It is as if this region lends itself to a sense of timelessness; where the elements are manifest in silent testimony of the greater universe; where a few visionary men and women have found the impetus, and the space, for their most cherished dreams and aspirations.

Karl Momen's Tree of Utah is no exception to the almost other-worldly influences that have played out in this barren wasteland, where the crew of the Enola Gay practiced their bombing runs before proceeding on to Hiroshima, and where members of the ill-fated Donner Party were tragically delayed before their awful demise in the Sierra Nevada mountains. It is into this heroic and severe environment that Momen introduced his bold and optimistic work; a work that carries with it echoes of anachronistic styles rooted in a distant world of Russian Constructivism, rediscovered in a new architectonic format. Ultimately it could be said that the Tree of Utah was created by an unlikely visitor from a foreign land, who, through his indomitable spirit and creative talent, paid a unique and unexpected tribute to the beauty of the Great Western Desert.

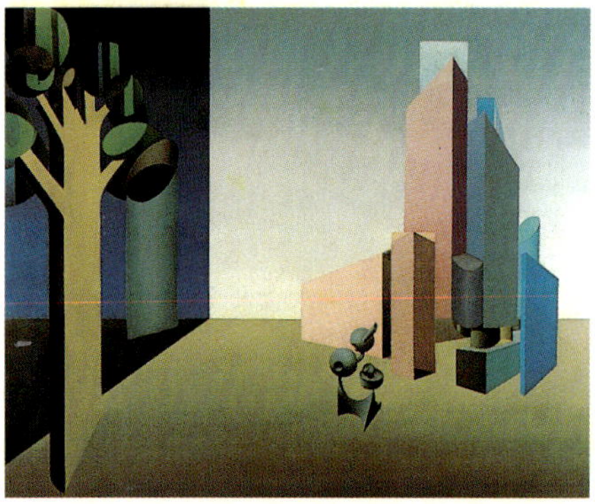

Structural Change, 1972 - 1978

Chapter one

A Bold and Propitious Talent

On a clear day the Tree of Utah is visible to travelers on Interstate 80 at a distance of 17 miles. It rises 87 feet high, stark and alone, as the highway cuts an arrow-straight line across the featureless surface of Utah's Great Western Desert. Motorists first see the multicolored spheres, as though suspended by invisible means above the desert. In warm weather the trunk is lost in the convection currents of hot air rising from the blanched desert floor; only the spheres shimmer mysteriously and silently in the arid atmosphere. On nearing the Tree, the trunk becomes visible and the spheres are elevated high above the surface, changing hue with the prevailing conditions of light and weather. Some commentators have referred to the Tree as the boldest piece of visual art to have been conceived in this conservative state. It has certainly become one of the most obtrusive public sculptures that few can ignore as they journey between Wendover on the Nevada border, and Salt Lake City. Not surprisingly it has also been the subject of considerable controversy. The debate surrounding the Tree has been complicated by the fact that the entire cost of this public sculpture was borne by the artist.

The physical dimensions of the Tree are impressive. As an expression of engineering virtuosity, it stands as an exemplar of the finest practice in pre-cast concrete construction. It is located adjacent to the westbound lane of Interstate 80 approximately 26 miles east of Wendover and 75 miles west of Salt Lake City. Towering above the salt flats, the structure was built to withstand desert winds of over 130 miles and hour, and earthquakes in the order of 7.5 on the Richter scale. The local Highway Patrol estimates that two million cars travel past the Tree annually and that five to seven cars an hour stop so occupants can view it—doing so is in violation of the law, as stopping along this highway is permitted only in cases of emergency. Because motorists have been known to doze off and not make it to their destination due to the monotony of traversing this barren, featureless landscape, this stretch of highway has become known by locals as the "Wendover Death Strip."

The curious onlooker may well ask what motivated the erection of such an apparently incongruous structure at this desolate site? The answer lies in the dream of its maker, Karl Momen, who had carved out a significant reputation for himself in Europe and Japan. He had held important solo exhibitions of his paintings and sculpture in New York, Stockholm, Tokyo, Berlin and Salt Lake City. Momen had also earned a reputation of being somewhat of a renegade in the art world, always ready to voice his nonalignment with the art cognoscente of the day. His idiosyncratic approach has its roots in his prodigious talent and his rich experience as an architect, painter, and sculptor in Europe after the demise of the Russian avant-garde. His formative career parallels the development of the modernist movement.

Momen was born in 1934 in Masshad, near the Russian border in Iran and was educated as an architect in Stuttgart in West Germany. He later became a resident and citizen of Sweden where he practiced architecture and developed his art under the dual influence of Nordic design principles and the aesthetics of Russian Constructivism. However, his real artistic roots go back to his youth. The youngest of a large family of brothers and sisters, he was the son of a designer and producer of Persian rugs. Momen's father produced many large carpets, supplying the Russian court and many dignitaries including Calouste Gulbenkian, the oil magnate, at the turn of the century. Some of these rare rugs can still be seen at the Gulbenkian Museum in Lisbon. The senior Momen eventually sold his business to the Iranian National Carpet Company but continued working as an expert consultant to the industry until his death at the advanced age of 104 years.

From an early age Momen was familiar with the Persian miniature paintings that decorated the walls of his parental home. He began to paint when he was seven years old. He discovered the studio of Name Piraste, a local painter in his hometown in Iran. He would hide outside Piraste's studio for hours on end, watching through the window, unnoticed, as the artist painted portraits and copies of famous European paintings from postcards and books. He became good friends with the painter who later taught him advanced painting techniques. When he was 8 years old a good friend of the family, Urie Popow, asked if he could give the young Momen art lessons. Popow had been an influential avant-garde painter in Russia before the Revolution. While he sold his more traditional work, and worked as an interior wall designer and decorator, Popow would paint one painting over another re-using the same canvas because he could not afford new canvases for his abstract work. During the time Momen studied with Popow he was introduced to the work of Kazimir Malevich (1878-1935), Vladimir Tatlin (1885-1953), El Lissitzky (1890-1941), as well as other Russian Constructivists and

Suprematists. He did not know who these painters were at the time and could not understand why they would paint abstract geometric images, but he was intrigued by their work nevertheless. Momen admits that he was particularly drawn to the work of El Lissitzky who, like himself, had also began his adult career as an architect.

Momen learned a great deal from Popow about the techniques of painting and he soon became a very skilled portraitist. As a young teenager he was assigned to copy 19th and early 20th century Russian paintings for the Soviet cultural center(VOX) in his hometown. He copied works of the Russian avant-garde painters including seminal works by Lyubov Popova (1889-1924), El Lissitzsky and Tatlin. Malevich's *Suprematist Composition: White on White* was one of the works rendered by the young Momen. At the age of 15 years he was commissioned to paint a six foot high official portrait of Stalin for civic celebration in his home town which had by this time fallen under Communist rule. Some years later when the Shah of Iran returned to power and Communism was denounced during the rule of Mossadegh, Momen watched as his portrait of Stalin was trampled under foot. Ironically, he was later commissioned to paint a similar portrait of the Shah of Iran, twelve feet high. History repeated itself when the Shah was denounced and Momen, who had left the country by this time, watched the destruction of this later portrait on television as troop carriers rolled over it in the street. For Momen this event graphically illustrated the fickleness of iconoclasm and the ephemeral nature of politically commissioned art.

In 1954 Momen completed his high school education, and proceeded to his military service at the military academy in Tehran. After his military training he traveled to Stuttgart, Germany, to begin his studies in architecture at the Kunst Academy. In 1958 he also gained admission to the art school where he befriended one of the teachers, a Professor Pheninger. He had supported himself in Iran by selling portraits and landscapes, and he continued this practice in Germany. At the Academy he was asked by Pheninger what he had hoped to learn, as his drawing, watercolor, and oil painting techniques were already so advanced. Ultimately Momen received more benefit from the long discussions he held with his teachers at the Academy about theoretical matters, than from studio practice.

A year later, as a student of the Academy, he attended the opening of an exhibition celebrating the work of Oskar Schlemmer (1888-1943), one of the founders of the Bauhaus. It was on this occasion that Pheninger introduced Momen to Max Ernst (1891-1975) as an unusual student who could employ ancient Persian miniature painting techniques in his watercolors. A longstanding friendship was established between the two men. Ernst was very interested in Persian miniatures and was intrigued with what Momen could reveal to him. Ernst in turn introduced Momen to the work that he and Jean Arp (1887-1966) were engaged in at the time. Ernst was occasionally a guest professor at the Academy, and Momen took full advantage of his visits. Momen was particularly interested in Ernst's approach to the expression of idea and emotion through art. Later Momen regretted that he had not spent more time with this visionary spirit. Several years later they met again in Stockholm when a large exhibition of Ernst's paintings from the Peggy Guggenheim collection opened at the Moderne Museet. Ernst was impressed with Momen's architectonic style and encouraged him not to be influenced by the trends of the art establishment. Momen took this advice to heart and has continued to work in his own idiosyncratic way ever since. Momen undertook his training in art and architecture, first in Germany and then in Sweden. For a while he worked on projects with the famed architect Le Corbusier (1888-1964). Momen immigrated to Sweden in 1961 with the intention of working on a six-month architectural project. He stayed and became a highly respected architect in Stockholm. By the 1980s he had given up his architectural work, devoting himself entirely to his art. At the time he was fully occupied supplying a waiting list of over forty European companies with paintings and sculptures produced under his hand. Momen quickly established a reputation for himself as a painter and sculptor in Europe, the US and Japan. He held important solo exhibitions in New York, Tokyo, Berlin, Stockholm, Monte Carlo, and Salt Lake City. His bronze sculptures were purchased predominantly by corporate customers in Europe, the US, and Japan. Although he had Swedish citizenship, he acquired a residence with a studio in Sausalito, California, where he could escape the severe Swedish winters. By the early 1990s his sculptures and paintings could be found in collections in such diverse places as Monte Carlo, and Brigham Young University in Provo, Utah. Significantly, almost all of Momen's sculptures—about 800 of them by the late 1980s—had been cast at a bronze foundry in Lehi, in Utah, under the supervision of Neil Hadlock, a former professor of sculpture at Brigham Young University and a sculptor in his own right. Momen had found that Hadlock's casting was equal to the finest European practice.

Karl Momen, the artist, is therefore the product of a unique synthesis of cosmopolitan influences that range from his earliest childhood memories of the Persian art of his parental home to his contact with the forms of early Russian avant-guard painting. He also fell under the spell of the Bauhaus through the work of Oskar Schlemmer which he greatly admired. He was well read and had opportunities to meet some of the most influential writers and painters who were also the pioneers of the modernist movement in Europe at the time.

Chapter two

THE DESERT VISION

Momen's affiliation to Utah began quite accidentally. At a news conference shortly after completion of the Tree of Utah, he exclaimed: "I did not pick Utah. Utah picked me!" The story of the Tree of Utah begins with Momen's journey across the breadth of the United States during the summer of 1981. He had decided to travel by car from Washington D.C. to the West Coast so that he could become better acquainted with the topography of the vast American landscape. After a week of cross-country driving he reached Salt Lake City on a sweltering August afternoon. With no local knowledge and no experience of the city's road numbering system he was soon frustrated in his attempts to find a hotel where he could stay the night. After giving up on his roadmap he found himself on the road to the airport where he conveniently checked in at the local Hilton hotel.

Momen found the hotel to be well appointed, and after the wearisome drive, most hospitable. However he was soon to be introduced to an important aspect of the local Mormon culture. When he tried to order a glass of wine, he was politely told by a courteous hotel attendant that he could procure the wine himself at the local newsstand! Momen complied. The following morning Momen was faced with two choices about which route he should take from hereon. He could take Interstate 15 and travel to Los Angeles via Las Vegas, or he could travel on Interstate 80 via Reno and Lake Tahoe to San Francisco. Notwithstanding an earlier interest in visiting Las Vegas, he chose to proceed on to San Francisco. Although it was only nine o'clock in the morning it was already hot and he stopped briefly to buy some tomatoes, lettuce, and ice as light refreshment for the long car journey ahead.

Momen soon left Salt Lake City far behind, and after an hour of uninterrupted trav-el, he became aware of the surreal desert landscape as he made his way along the dead straight highway to his first rest stop at the border town of Wendover. The desert heat and blazing sun would have been unbearable but for the air-conditioned environment of the car. The thought occurred to him that it was as though he was driving over a gigantic blanched canvas. The straight road disappeared toward the horizon and the heat eddies in the air obliterated the distant mountains. He felt as if he was driving through unlimited white space, almost as though he had left the planet. After a while Momen reached into the back for one of the tomatoes and some lettuce he had bought for light refreshment before he had left the city that morning and it occurred to him that he did not have salt for his tomato. The thought crossed his mind that he could wait until he reached Wendover where he would be able to buy some salt. Then it dawned on him that he was traversing the largest dried salt lake in the world with what appeared to be endless expanses of the white substance in every direction!

Momen stopped on the shoulder of the road, got out of the vehicle, and was immediately blasted by the searing hot air. It was as if he had opened the door into an oven. As he walked over the white surface his shoes crunched the salt and he reflected on the fact that it was not unlike powder snow, but for the 120-degree temperature difference! He stooped down, took a pinch of the white powder and ate the tomato with some haste, fearing that it might get scorched in the inferno of hot air and reflected heat that rose from the white terrain. After taking in the alien panorama for a moment or two, Momen returned to the welcome air-conditioned comfort of his vehicle and resumed his journey.

As the journey progressed he watched as tiny black dots in the distance grew into large vehicles, just to disappear again as they whooshed past on the dead straight eastbound lane of the highway. Then the thought struck him that the monotony of this seemingly endless journey could be relieved by some reference point in the desert — some focus of color that would arrest the eye amidst this wide expanse of featureless terrain. Momen's thoughts raced ahead of himself—the car, the endless sea of salt, the emptiness of the barren terrain. He felt a surge of inspiration as he contemplated the possibility of superimposing some element of color upon that sterile environment as a reference point for the eye, and perhaps for the entire soul. And who better to do it than he the artist! Thoughts and images flashed through his mind as he realized the potential of his musings. He felt as if he was on the verge of a unique and powerful new discovery. Something had to be done—but what? Suddenly, he found himself entering the outskirts of Wendover. Momen continued his journey on to Reno, where he would rest from driving. However, that night as he lay in his hotel room, images of that morning's poignant experience on Interstate 80 kept flashing through his mind.

The next morning Momen continued his journey; then, some time before he reached San Francisco, he stopped the car on the side of the road and penciled a preliminary sketch of what was to become the Tree of Utah. He had envisioned a large structure,

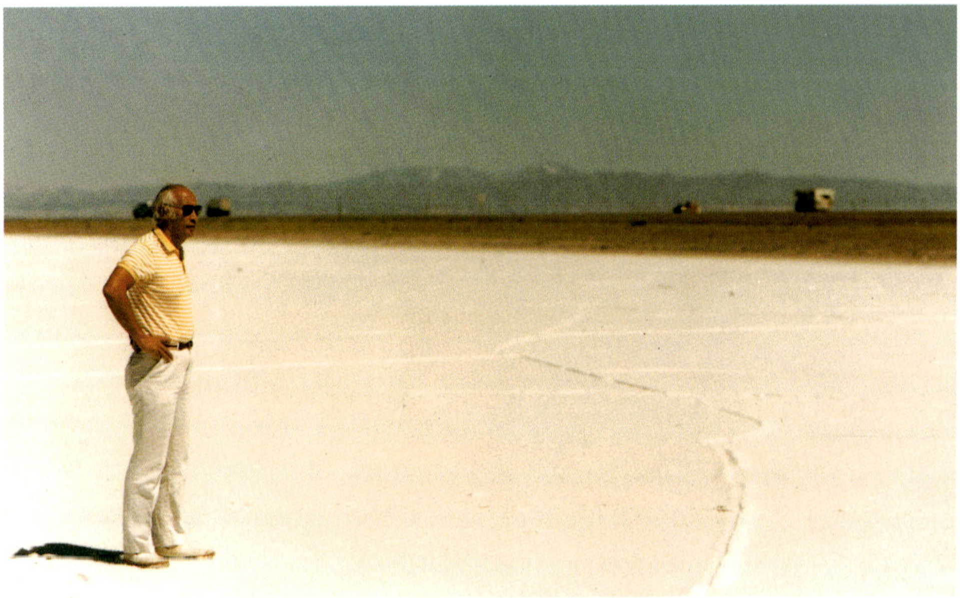

Momen surveying the wide open expanse of desert near Wendover prior to construction of the Tree.

symbolic of a tree that rose from the desert and visible for miles around. The image was not unlike the characteristic tree symbol he had previously used in his paintings. The tree held its characteristic spheres high above the flat terrain like fantastical fruit in full bloom. On reaching San Francisco he reached into his bags and pulled out one of his lithographs that contained an earlier image of his tree symbol. He cut out the image and used it to make a three-dimensional collage depicting the tree rising adjacent to the highway on a topographical map of the desert. This simple exercise, in itself illustrates the importance that Momen accorded the setting of the work within a specific landscape.

The "Tree" is defined in terms of its proximity to the road that cuts an arrow-straight line across the featureless desert. The "Tree" is to be "read" in terms of these simple but inextricably related elements. We are reminded of an idea contained in one of the anonymous slogans that was used at the exhibition of Tatlin's tower in Petrograde: "By realizing the form of the large space, we are overcoming the form."[1] In the full realization of Constructivist theory there occurred a transition from experimentation with mere abstract form, to the analysis of real elements of the physical and spatial environment. We see this aspect manifest in the development of Momen's thinking towards the realization of his concept of the "Tree" as a concrete construction located adjacent to a road in the desert. This realization goes beyond the placing of a visual element against a background or "foil" that would qualify it in terms of the simple figure/ground relationship of a Gestalt composition. (See Chapter 8 for a more complete treatment of the influence of Constructivist principles on Momen's aesthetic sensibility).

Rather, we see the full realization of the concept in terms of a real world solution that takes into account the spatial elements of a vast landscape. We are also reminded of the statement contained in the Realist Manifesto: "The realization of our perceptions of the world in the forms of space and time is the only aim of our pictorial and plastic art."[2] The "Objectivist" Working Group INKhUK similarly stated that "the group is working not on the representation of elements, but the creation of a concrete organism both in space and on surfaces."[3] These views are further reinforced by Aleksandr Vesnin's "Credo" in which he states: "Clearly the objects created by the contemporary artist must be pure constructions untrammeled by pictorial representation, constructed on the principle of the straight line and the geometrical curve, and as economically as possible for a given maximum effort."[4] From its very inception Momen's "Tree" complies with the theoretical stances about non-representation and the creation of concrete objects as the only solution to the artist's dilemma of how to impinge upon his, or her, environment.

References.

1. Anatlii Strigalev "The Art of the Constructivists: From Exhibition to Exhibition, 1914-1932" in *Art Into Life: Russian Constructivism, 1914-1932*, edited by Richard Andrews. Rizzoli, New York, 1990, p.31
2. Naum Gabo, Noton Pevsner, *Realistic Manifesto*, Second State Printing House, August 5, 1920, Document from a private collection published in *Art Into Life: Russian Constructivism, 1914-1932*, edited by Richard Andrews. Rizzoli, New York, 1990. P.12
3. Document from a private collection published in ed., Richard Andrews, *Art Into Life: Russian Constructivism, 1914-1932*, Rizoli, New York, 1990, p.12. 4 Ibid. p. 68.
4. Ibid. p.68

Chapter three

NEW FRIENDSHIPS AND ALLIANCES

In San Francisco Momen became increasingly excited about his vision for a large structure in the Great Western desert, but he had no idea who he should talk to about it, or who the responsible authorities might be that would have jurisdiction over such a project. After some inquiries he was referred to the Utah Arts Council. He telephoned the Council in early September 1981 and spoke with Ruth Draper and Arley Curtz who were the director and assistant director, respectively, at the time. The Utah Arts Council distributes funds that are received for the arts by both the Utah State Legislature and the National Endowment for the Arts. The Council had been active in providing for outreach services to schools, local arts councils, community centers, performing groups, and to individual Utah artists. The Council also had a mandate to act as a state coordinator and advisor in bringing the arts to the people of Utah.

After his initial contact with Curtz and Draper, Momen was asked to mail them a written proposal for his project for consideration by the Council. He immediately went to work and produced a small maquette and perspectival drawings depicting the "Tree" as he had envisioned it adjacent to the highway near Wendover. Then, with the model under his arm, he boarded the first flight to Salt Lake City and within hours he was speaking face-to-face with Draper and Curtz—only two days after his initial telephone call to them from San Francisco. Somewhat incredulously they ushered Momen into the first floor conference room of the Arts Council where he proceeded to present his idea with the aid of the maquette and drawings he had brought with him. He was to revisit this room many times over the next several years as the project evolved. At this initial meeting Draper and Curtz found it hard to accept that this stranger, with whom they had only spoken briefly on the telephone a few days previously, was so seriously committed to such an unusual undertaking. The members of the Utah Arts Council were excited

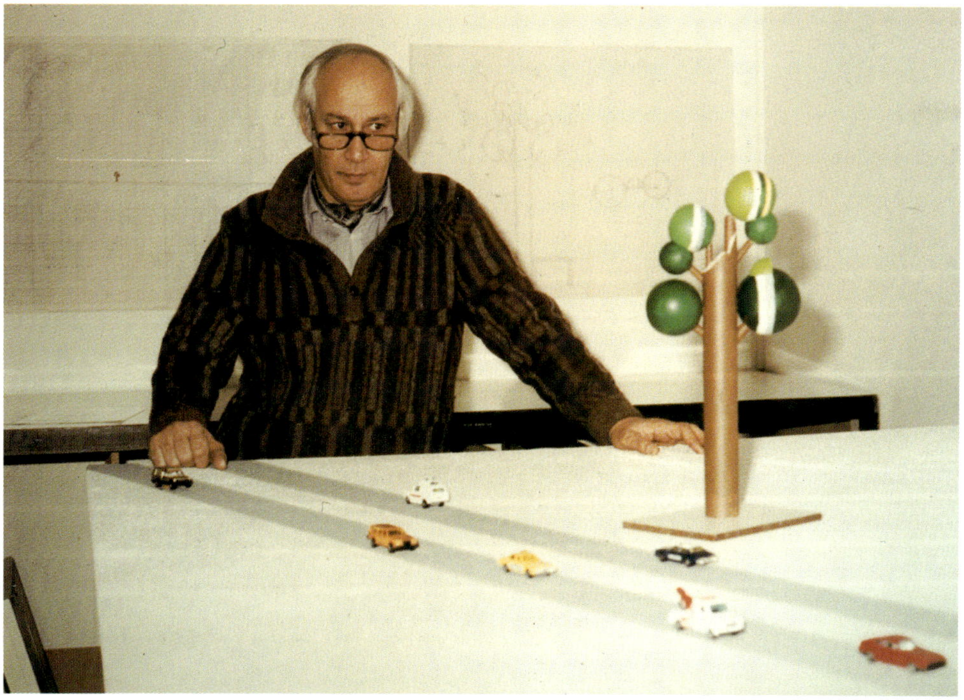

Momen with the small maquette indicating the position of the Tree adjacent to Interstate Highway 80.

about the project and Curtz sent Momen an encouraging letter offering the Council's assistance whereupon Momen returned to Sweden to give the technical aspects of the project serious consideration and to consult with engineering colleagues. He now turned his thoughts to the shape and size of the final design. In the initial architectural design of the project he envisioned a structure between 75 and 85 feet high. The international news media wasted no time in publicizing Momen's proposal for a large sculpture in the mid-western American desert. The project received immediate attention in Swedish television news broadcasts. Photographs of Momen's model for the project were publicized far and wide. In April 1982 a public announcement about the initiation of the project was made at the Berlin Cultural Center in Germany. At a special reception the director of the Center presented Momen with a 10 foot high cake shaped in the form of the "Tree." The following day the event made national and international headlines and Momen knew, for better or worse, he was committed to the project and that from that day on, he could not allow himself to back out of it.

In the fall of 1982, not long after this enthusiastic reception in Europe, Momen received a chilling letter from the Utah Arts Council informing him that they were distancing themselves from his project. Although they would not stand in his way, they would also not be able to give him any material assistance. The Council would adopt a neutral stance toward the project. Upon receiving this disconcerting news Momen immediately returned to Salt Lake City to discuss the matter with Draper, Curtz, and

Dennis Smith, the Chairman of the Visual Art Committee of the Arts Council. Although Smith had resisted Momen's ideas initially, he soon warmed to Momen's enthusiasm. After a subsequent meeting, Smith agreed that, although the Council would not be able to give any material assistance, they would act in a consultative capacity offering advice and general guidance as the project developed. Smith was one of the only members of the Council who supported Momen's proposal. Momen grew to respect Smith as a sculptor and for the good work that he was doing to promote the arts in the State. He was to establish an abiding friendship with Smith over subsequent years.

Undaunted by this lukewarm response from the Utah Arts Council, Momen resolved that he would "go it alone" and turned his attention to the first priority in getting the project started—securing a site for his sculpture. Dennis Smith accompanied Momen to a meeting with representatives of the Utah Land Board. At this meeting he was informed that, as he was not an American citizen, he would not be able to purchase land in the area due to the strategic location of the site, which was in close proximity to two U.S. Air Force bases. This argument was brought into sharp focus by Momen's observation that he had recently purchased a condominium in Washington D.C. not far from the White House! However, the Land Board representatives referred Momen to Khosrow Semnani, a local businessman who owned large tracts of land in this arid region as one who might be able to help him.

Although Momen was scheduled to fly out of Salt Lake that evening, he was able to arrange a meeting with Semnani before his departure. At Semnani's offices in downtown

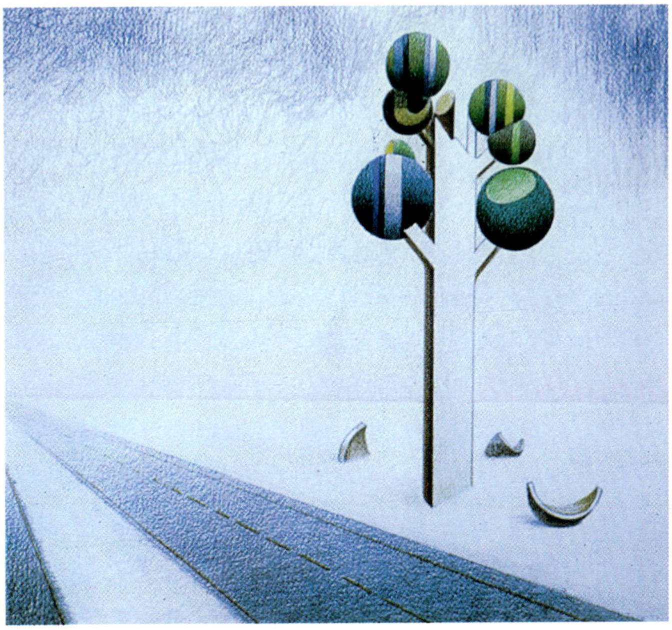

An early drawing by Momen while the project was still in the planning stages. Pastel

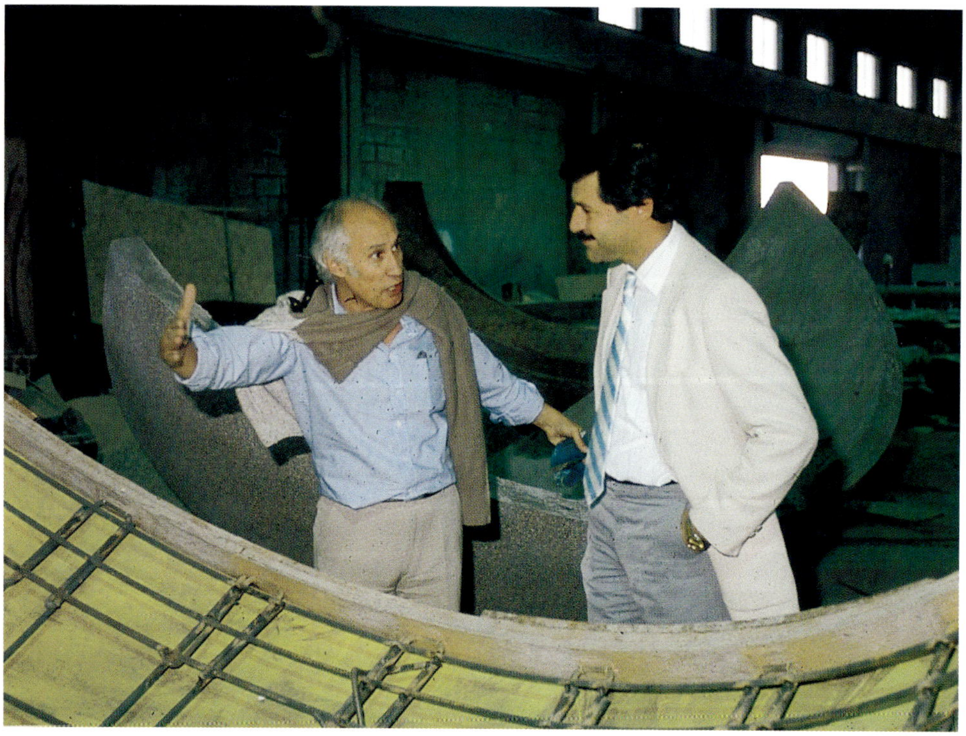

Momen shows a section of one of the large spherical molds to Khosrow Semnani (right) in Don Reimann's factory.

Salt Lake City, Momen was graciously received and, after lengthy and wide-ranging conversation, Momen showed Semnani his model and the drawings for the Tree of Utah. Semnani was intrigued by the idea and after further discussion he generously offered to sponsor the project to the extent of providing a plot of land for the site of the sculpture. Although the particular site in Tooele County that Momen had earmarked for the sculpture belonged to the State Board of Education, Semnani was able to arrange a trade involving other parcels of land that he owned in the area. At the conclusion of their meeting, as Momen and Semnani were bidding each other farewell, they discovered to their mutual amazement that they were both of Iranian parentage and that they were both fluent in Pharse, their mother tongue. Upon realization of this most unlikely coincidence, Semnani pledged even greater assistance to Momen for his project. Ultimately, Momen would come to rely heavily on the magnanimous support of Semnani for the completion of the sculpture.

Back in Sweden, Momen continued to communicate with Dennis Smith of the Utah Art Council. On his return to Utah in the middle of March 1983, Semnani had completed his transactions in securing a suitable site for the structure. Local newspapers were quick to report on the initial plans for the project. The Salt Lake Tribune of March 20,

1983 ran the first comprehensive local article about the project after interviewing Momen and Dennis Smith about their plans. Numerous visits were made to the local county planning commission and to the Utah Land and Forestry Division for specific permits and approvals. Momen again returned to Sweden to prepare the final architectural drawings for the project. On his return in the fall of 1983, Momen had detailed drawings for the sculpture. During this early period Semnani facilitated the project by assisting Momen in preparing the numerous applications and submissions to the various authorities to obtain the necessary permits for the structure. After several meetings with representatives of the board of directors of Tooele County, the project accelerated. By October Momen had called for tenders for the construction of the structure from several local construction companies. He received three estimates which ranged from $300,000 to $500,000, but no one could give him a firm estimate as no one, at this stage, knew the condition of the soil at the site. In working with the various local authorities, Momen soon discovered that there were mixed feelings in the community about his project. Some people were enthusiastic and very helpful, while others were quite negative and even resentful about his plan to erect a structure in the desert. Late in October 1983, Momen received a construction proposal from Don Reimann, a Salt Lake City contractor with a company by the name of Style Crete. Reimann had a reputation as the finest concrete caster in the state. The Reimann family had been in the stone casting business since the Mormon pioneers entered the Salt Lake valley in the mid-1800s. Reimann ran a family business with his eight sons and had worked on a variety of imposing structures, including the large ZCMI department store building in downtown Salt Lake City, as well as temple buildings for the Church of Jesus Christ of Latter-day Saints in Ogden and Provo. Moreover, Reimann was one of the few contractors in the world who was prepared to undertake the challenge of casting concrete spheres over thirteen feet in diameter. At a meeting in Semnani's office in Salt Lake City, Momen met Reimann and one of his sons John, who was completing an architecture degree at the University of Utah at the time. Reimann was intrigued by the project and expressed his interest in doing the work. He was particularly interested in involving John, as he thought that the project would provide an excellent opportunity for his son to gain valuable practical experience working on a project of such an unusual nature. When Momen needed a structural engineer, Don Reimann recommended Devon Stone, of Midvale, for the job. Stone reviewed Momen's architectural drawings and expressed the opinion that he did not think it a very difficult project, that it had some challenges, but that it was possible. Reimann agreed to work with Stone in producing the structural plans. Within a month all their calculations had been completed and the party met again in Salt Lake City. Although Momen was keen to sign an agreement with Reimann at that time in order to get the work under way, Reimann deferred until he could make some final calculations. In his eagerness to move the work along Momen gave a deposit of money to Semnani who acted as the facilitator to all the negotiations at the time, and Semnani in turn, gave a preliminary good faith payment to Reimann early in January 1984. Final plans were sent to various authorities in Tooele County and a building permit for the "Tree" was granted at the end of that month.

At this point Momen and Reimann agreed to draw up a contract for the completion of the structure. The contract price proposed by Reimann was $385,000. However, while Reimann was having the contract reviewed by his uncle, Ralph Klemp an attorney at law, Momen decided he could not procrastinate any longer and started ordering materials. Ultimately Reimann agreed to work for labor and construction costs and Momen undertook to purchase the materials. With the legalities of the construction finalized, all the local authorities appeased, and a fine team assembled, Momen took a permanent suite at the Hilton hotel in Salt Lake City to oversee the project. With his characteristic and finely tuned sense of the dramatic, Momen hired Frank Harris, a cameraman from Los Alamos to document the construction process. Soon Harris and his wife were engaged in filming the preparations for the "Tree" at Reimann's warehouse in Salt Lake City on a daily basis.

Chapter four

CHALLENGES

Artistic projects of the size and complexity of the Tree of Utah are prone to problems that could arise at any time during the production process. These difficulties are usually the result of unforeseen circumstances that seem to manifest themselves whenever innovative solutions are sought for unique situations. Art works are, by definition, unique and original, and their production often involves the use of new materials or methods that test the boundaries of conventional practice. There are often no precedents to refer to and new practices are established in accordance with needs as they arise. From the outset the construction of Momen's Tree of Utah was fraught with uncertainties about the materials and technical specifications of the structure and environmental factors associated with its desert location. These uncertainties had financial repercussions, and costs increased as ways were found to overcome unforeseen contingencies. No one had ever built such an unusual pre-cast concrete sculpture in such a hostile environment, at such a remote location in this state before. Momen had limitations to the amount of money he could raise from his own resources. Sponsorships were not forthcoming from private or corporate donors and funding for the project from the state's arts council was non-existent. The eventual cost of the project would fall mightily on Momen's shoulders. Little did he know, at the time, the degree to which his personal resolve and his limited financial resources would be strained in the months ahead. Momen's artistic integrity would also be tested by the physical limitations and restrictions imposed by environmental factors in the construction of the Tree. Overcoming these factors would present daunting challenges to his personal resolve and his financial resourcefulness.

Although Momen had some preliminary work done in California to determine if such a structure was feasible, no clear set of technical specifications had been provided for the construction of the Tree. Momen's first proposal was for a structure 45 to 50 feet in height. The Tree finally ended up rising to more than 80 feet above the desert floor. This was almost twice the dimension of the original estimates and impacted dramatically on the projected cost of the project. As the dimensions of a pre-cast concrete structure are increased, so the cost of the project increases at an exponential rate. Although the first scale model of the Tree indicated only five colors, the finished structure ended up with more than 30 different colors. These upward revisions of the overall specifications of the work were to result in serious financial problems for Momen later in the project.

One of the most important considerations that occupied the minds of both Momen and Reimann at the outset of the construction was the choice of surface finish for the spheres. Each of the large concrete spheres was to receive a decorative finish in keeping with Momen's overall design concept of the work. In the absence of anything better at the time, Momen and Reimann had considered using ceramic tiles. Tiles were not a satisfactory solution as they would crack and break over time. Environmental conditions were harsh in the desert with wide-ranging extremes of temperature that could result in fractures of the material due to constant expansion and contraction.

During March 1984, after lengthy discussions and inquiries about numerous materials, both men concluded that anhydrous copper silicate, commonly known as chrysocolla, had the technical properties and the ideal coloration for their purpose. Moreover, this material was indigenous to Utah! The blue and green rocks were quarried in southern Utah near Milford, a desert town about 500 miles south of Salt Lake City. The market value of the rock was usually two dollars a pound and used by the Native American people in the region to make jewelry. Reimann contacted the owners of the quarry who agreed to donate one hundred tons of the stone to the project. However, Reimann and his team would have to quarry and transport the rock themselves. In mid-March 1984 Reimann and his eight sons traveled down to southern Utah. The Reimanns made a family activity of this project, and included a number of grandchildren. On arrival at the site in a remote desert location the party found the deserted and disused quarry. The mining company had taken what they could from the hard dry earth and all that remained were a series of large open pits, a hundred to two hundred feet in diameter and of equal depth. The only evidence of the sought after chrysocolla were the blue-green seams that jutted out around the walls of the pits. To make matters worse, the best stone was located about half way down the walls of the cavernous excavations, often a hundred feet above the pit floor, and in the most inaccessible locations. The stone within easy reach was immediately attacked with hammers and chisels. However, this source was soon exhausted and the men turned their attention to the better rocks that protruded from the sides of the vertical walls, high above their heads. However, there

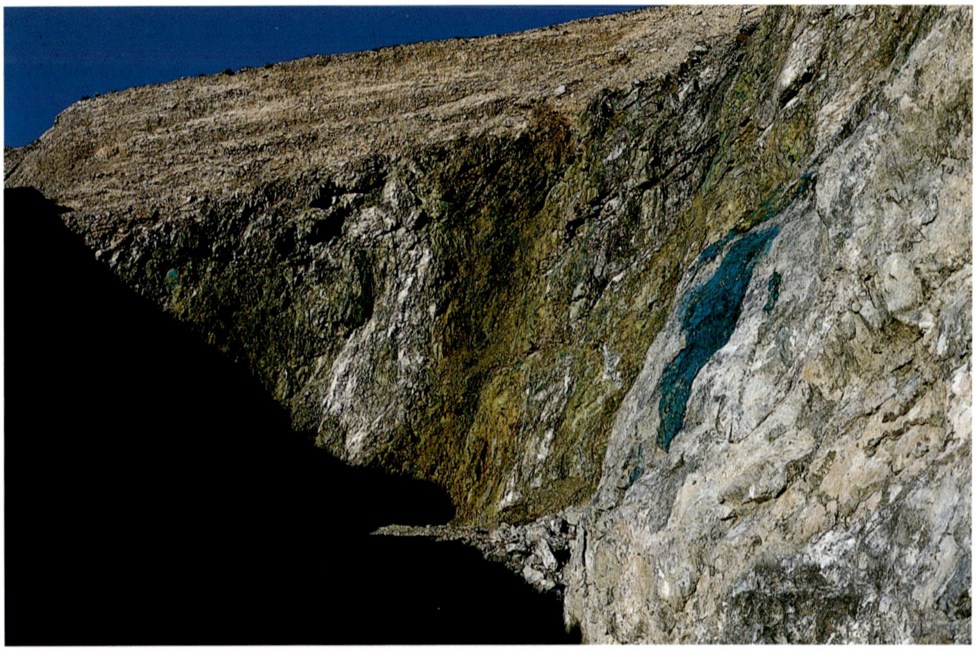

The cavernous opencast mine near Milford, in southern Utah were Reimann and his team quarried copper silicate for the surface covering of the spheres.

appeared to be no way that Reimann's gang could get to them. Undaunted, Reimann reached for the powerful 300 Weatherby Magnum rifle that he often carried on such excursions, took careful aim at an outcrop of the chrysocolla stone, and blasted a sizable chunk of rock to the ground. He soon found this method to be too tedious and also very hard on the shoulder.

Undaunted, he resorted to another plan. Reimann drove his four-wheel-drive vehicle to an overhang above one of the pits and lowered his sons down the sheer rock-face with ropes and cables attached to the vehicle's winch. One of Reimann's sons, John, was an exceptionally strong young man and had previously set a bench press record of 580 pounds at his high school. Standing upright with one foot in the loop of the cable, John was lowered down into the cavern. He clutched the cable with his left hand while he swung at the rock face with a pinchbar that he held in his right hand. As individual stones were levered and broken from the walls by the team they fell crashing and clattering to the desert floor below. Reimann's grandchildren later had great fun in retrieving the rocks and throwing them onto the two large diesel trucks; this was an adventure for them that they would long remember. Reimann's team spent three days quarrying in this fashion. When sufficient material had been accumulated, the party packed up, and the load was hauled back to Salt Lake City. Momen was extremely satisfied with the successful completion of this exercise. The stone was the perfect material for his purpose. Back in Salt Lake City a stone cutter was immediately contracted to cut the stone pieces to size with a diamond saw. However, good fortune and

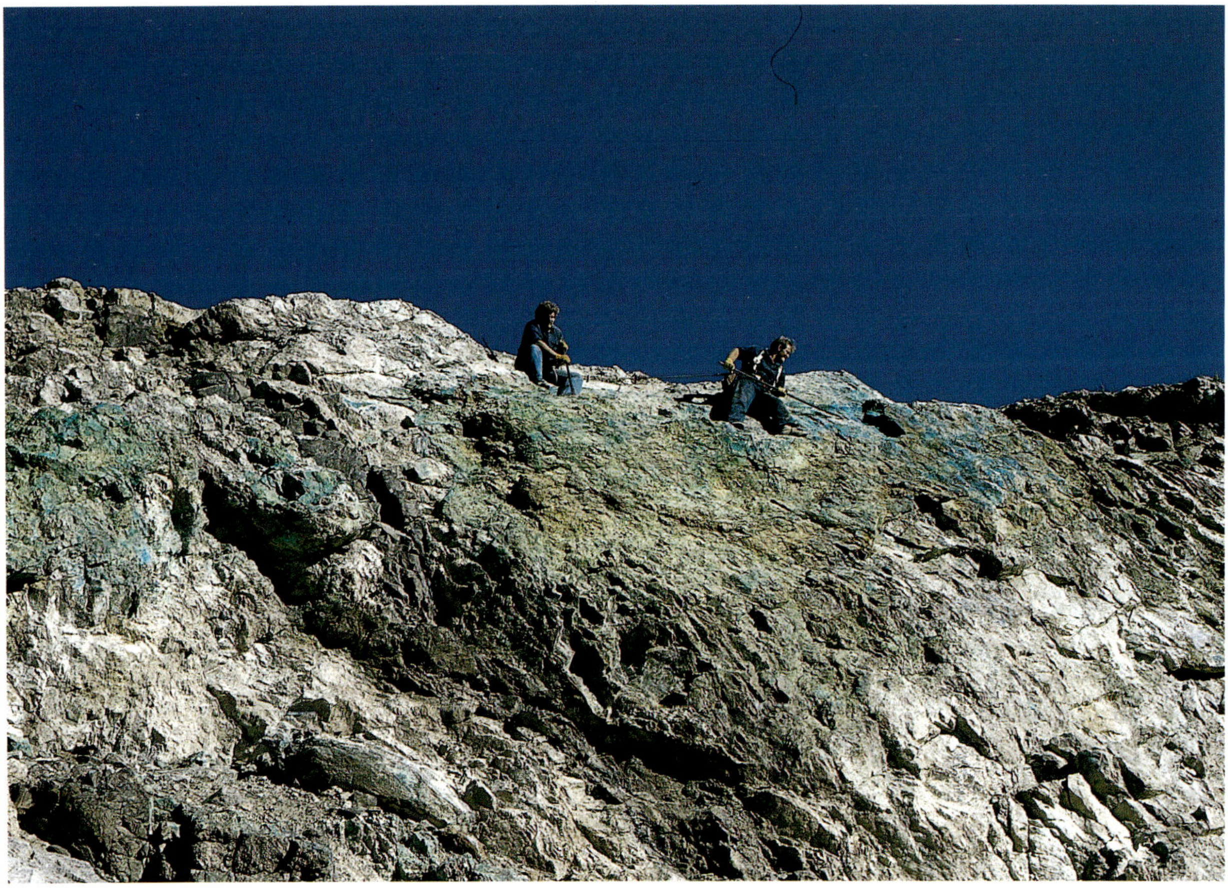

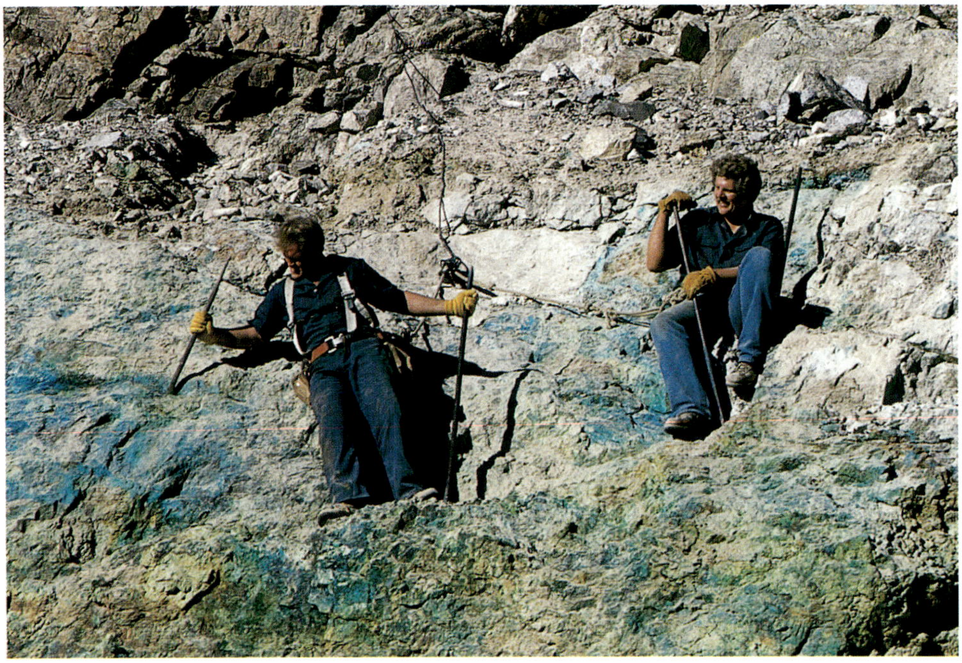

Top: *Don Reimann's team at the edge of the quarry wall.*

Left: *Brett and Gary Reimann levering chrysocolla from the rock face with crowbars.*

Right: *One of the large trucks laden with chrysocolla prior to returning to Salt Lake City.*

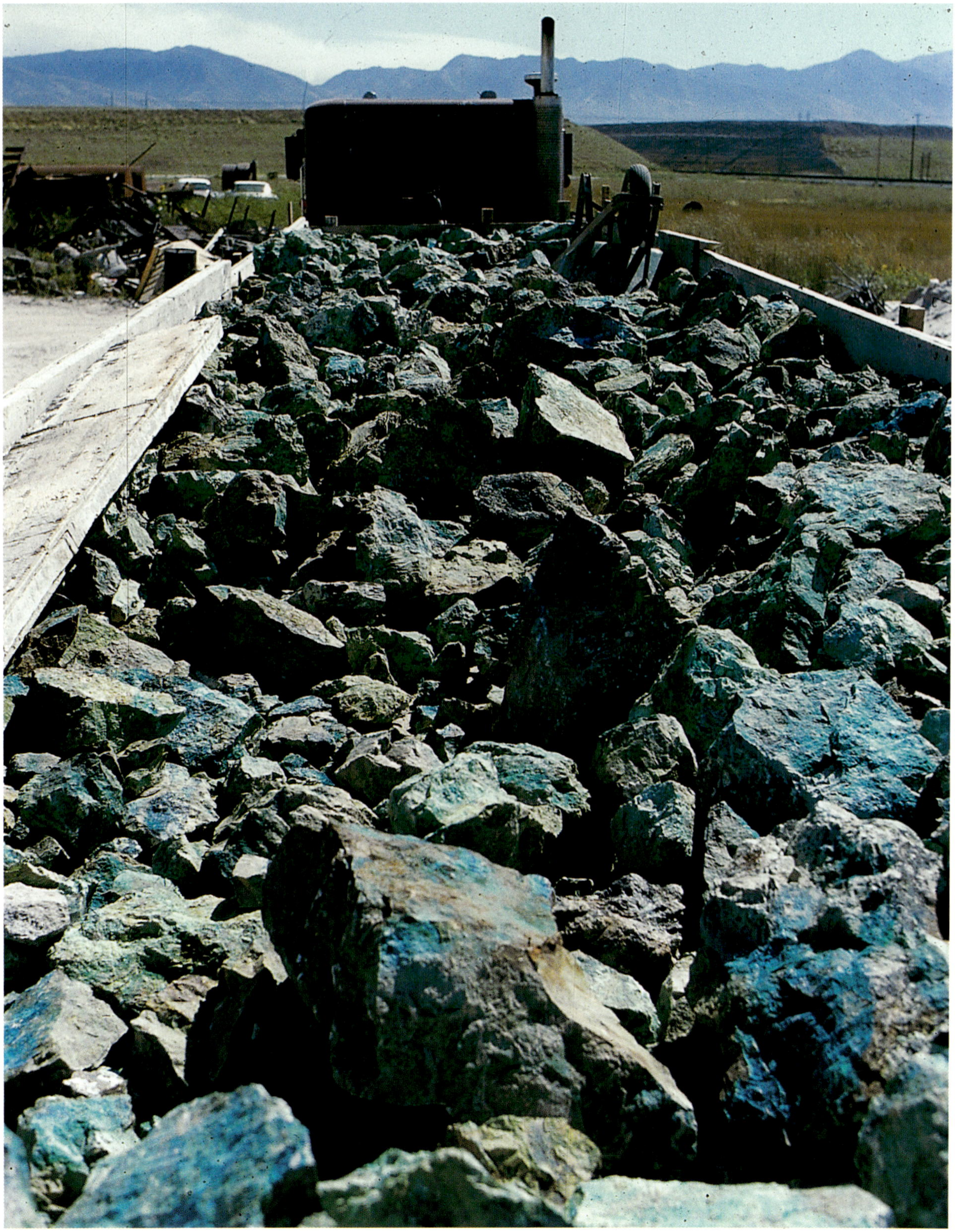

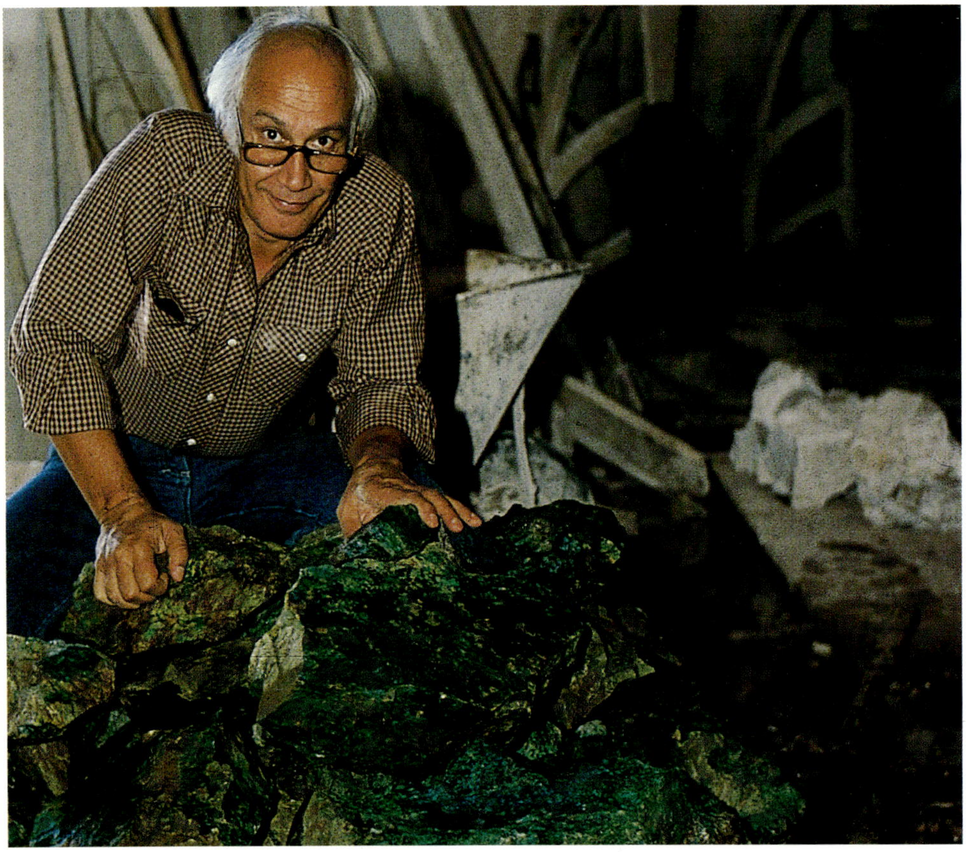

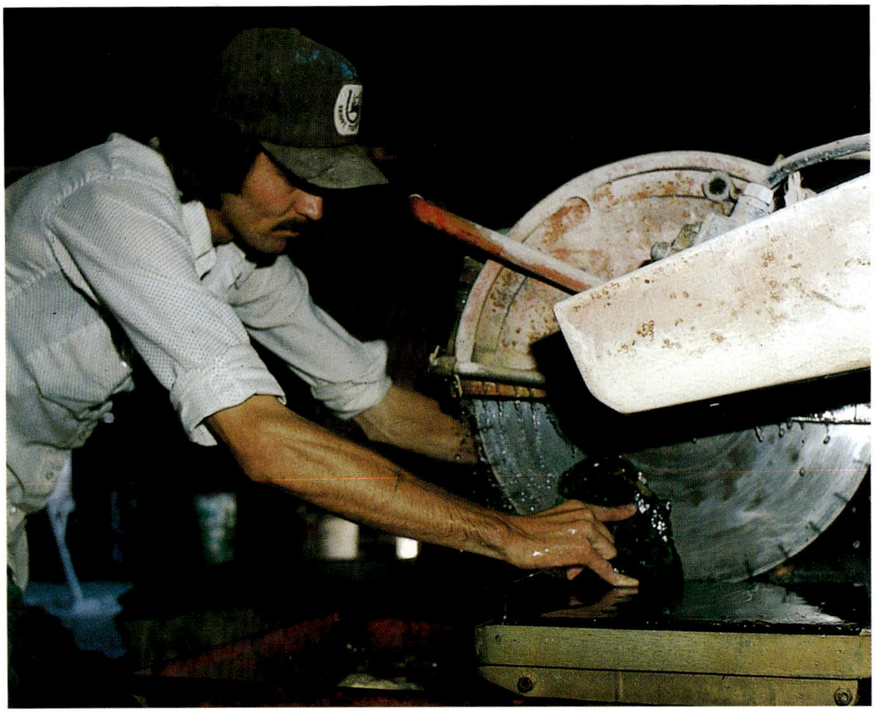

Top: *Momen inspecting the chrysocolla rocks after the successful expedition to southern Utah.*

Left: *Cutting the rocks with a diamond saw.*

Right: *Examples of the rocks that werer later cut into more regular shapes siutable for adhering to the surfaces of the spheres.*

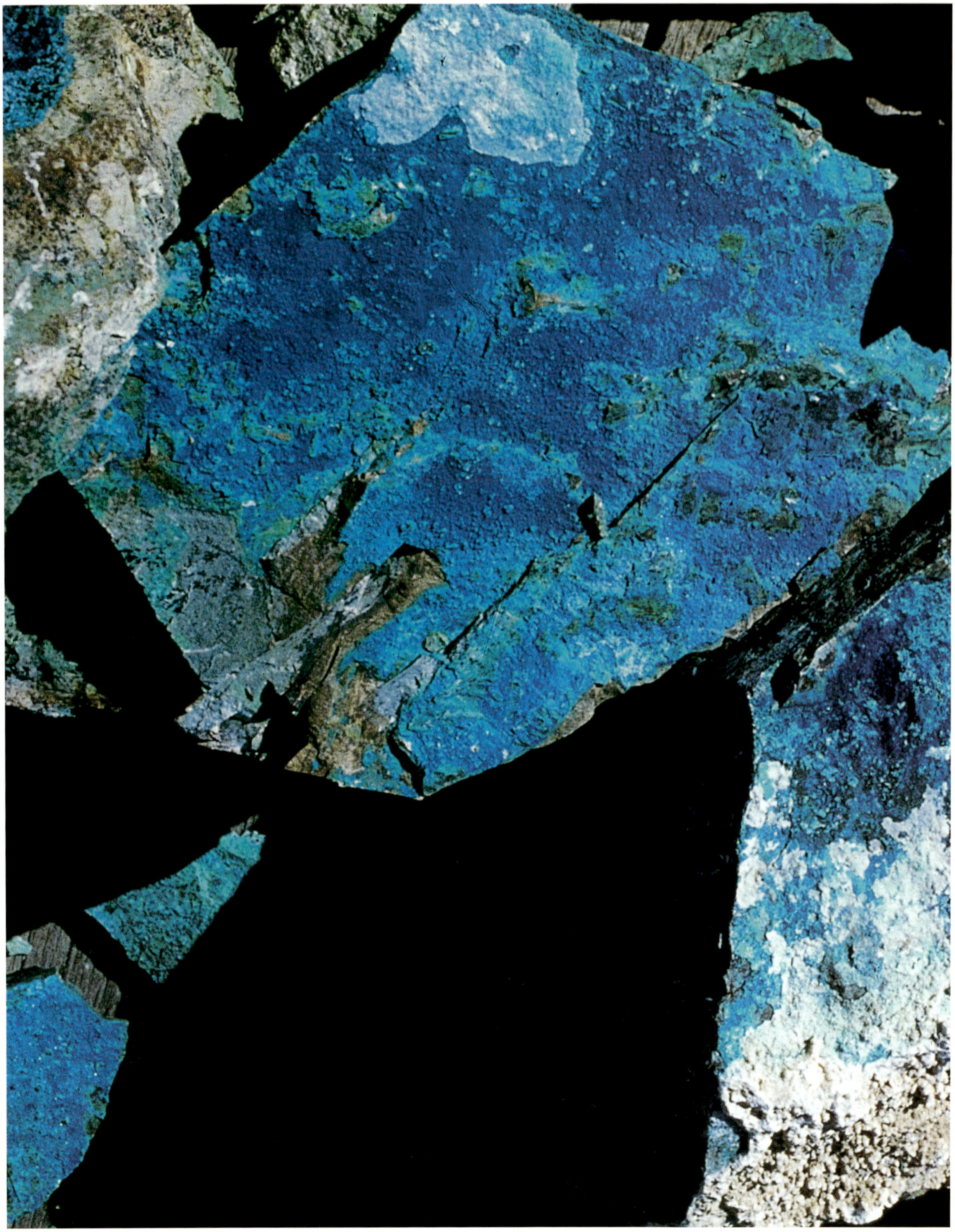

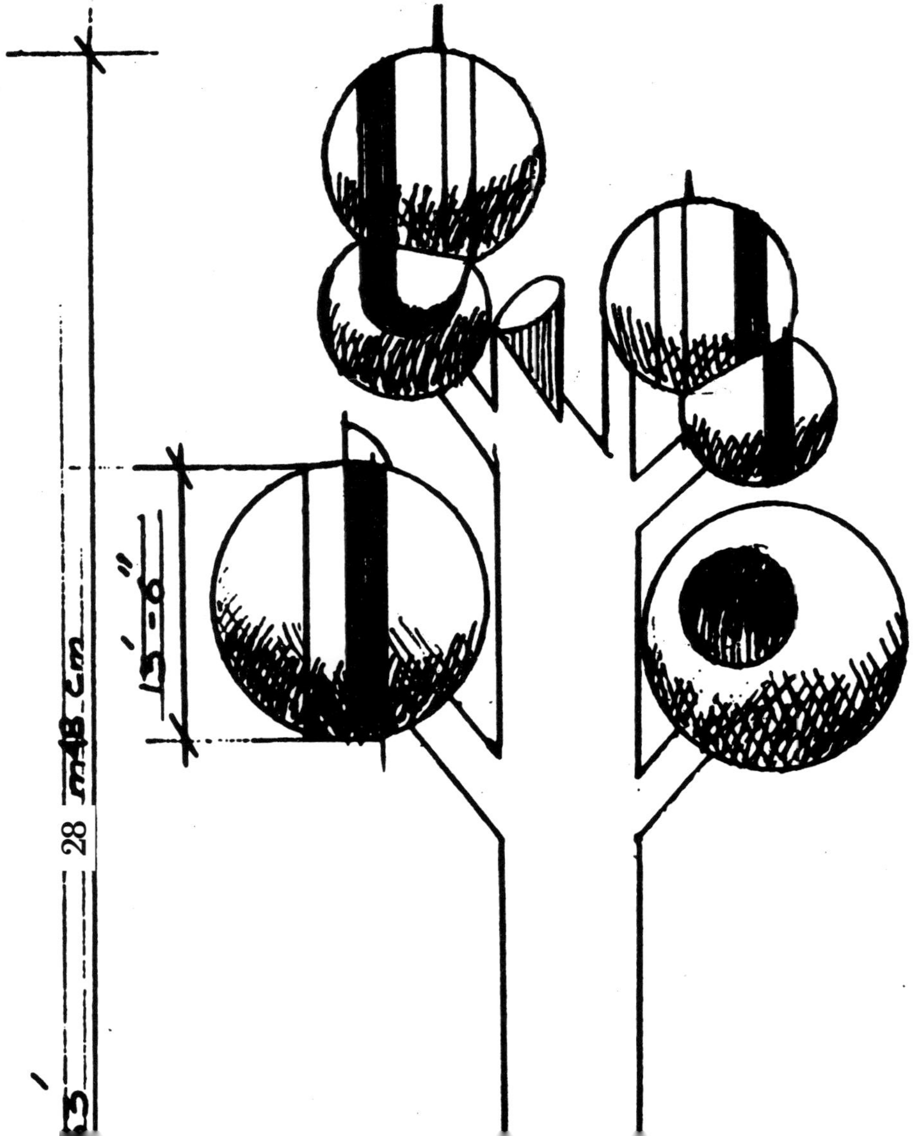

SPECIFICATION

COLORED ROCKS MARBLE GRANITE DIO. PSIDE . CHRYSACOLLA, ANHYDROS SILICATE OF COPPER.	90	TONS
EPOXY	4	"
STEEL	160	"
COLORED CEMENT	15	"
CEMENT & SAND	255	"
CERAMIC 18.000 PIECES		
WELDING RODS	5	"
WOOD FOR MOLDS	7	"

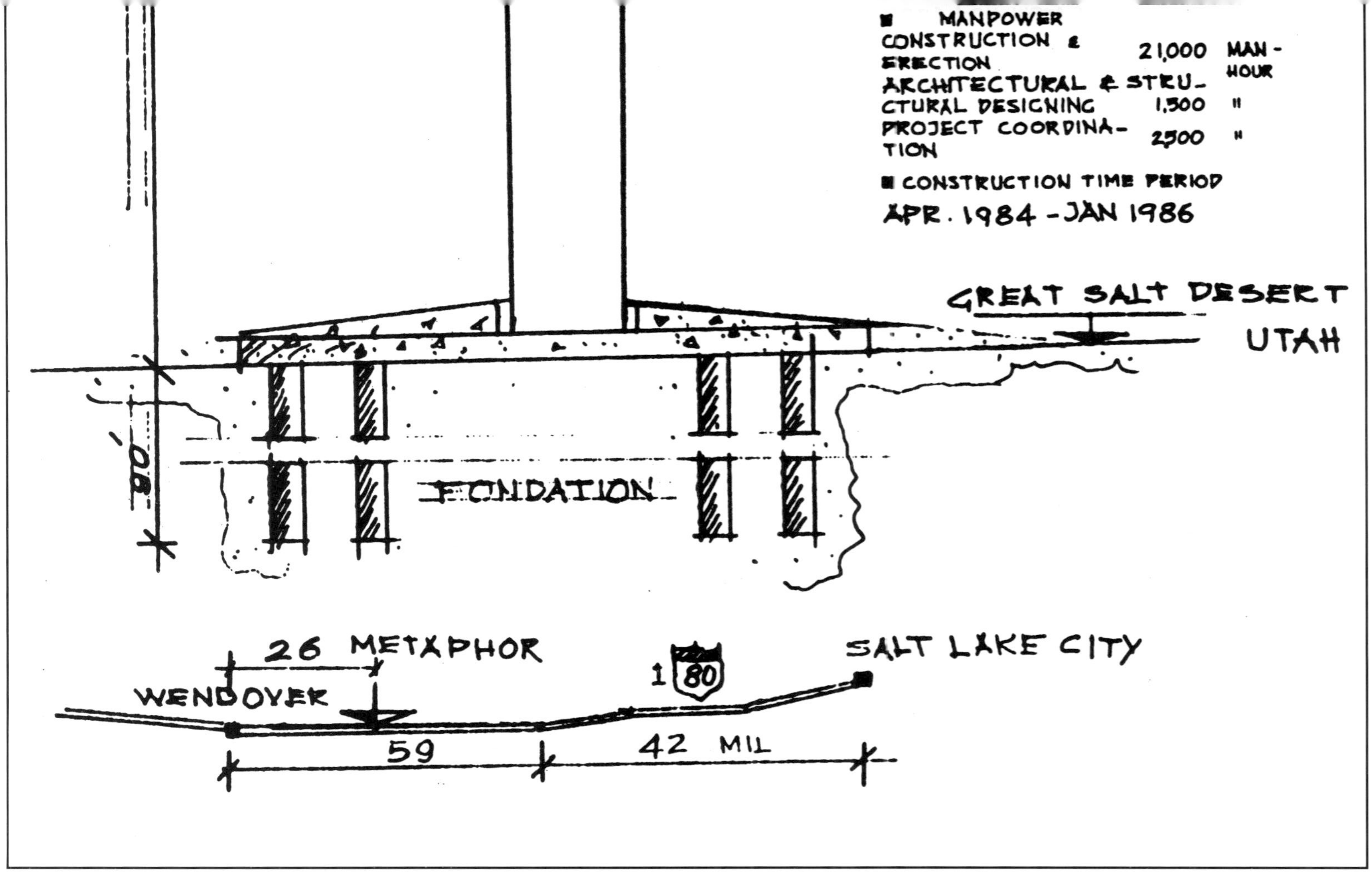

Momen's elevation drawing of the Tree indicating the massive foundation of concrete piles below the deseert floor. At this time (1984) Momen had contemplated naming the Tree "Metaphor" alluding to its symbolism. The exact site of construction is indicated as 26 miles east of Wendower, adjacent to Interstate Highway 80, in the Great Western Desert.

propitious circumstances were soon to be over-shadowed by some of the most demanding challenges that Momen had ever faced in his career.

The plans for the structure called for large concrete spheres, of considerable weight, hanging from a central trunk. Reimann had never built anything like this before and he was still unsure of whether it would be possible to build the structure that Momen had dreamed of. However, after a structural engineer was hired, Reimann changed his mind. Devon Stone produced careful calculations that indicated the technical specifications that would make the Tree a reality. Reimann breathed a sigh of relief and gained renewed confidence in his ability to complete the project. These initial calculations were to be revised and modified throughout the period of construction; the entire concept of what was to be built became ever clearer as new calculations were made, and the work got underway. These changes revealed an organic process of action and corresponding reaction as ongoing corrections were made to adapt working methods and materials to the needs of the evolving artwork. There are no clear formulas or ready-made recipes for innovative art—each work has to be resolved in terms of its own intrinsic structural and aesthetic exigencies. The strengths of materials, sheer factors, and load bearing considerations are all subservient factors and become the means to realize the artist's vision. A fine work of art will stand independently of any design considerations, as a whole, and will always be greater than the sum of its fabrication techniques and material specifications.

Momen and Reimann's relief was short-lived. A few months into the project, it was discovered that the amount of steel reinforcing that would be required had been under estimated. New calculations by Devon Stone indicated that the final weight of the piece would far exceed the one hundred tons originally estimated. It was also at this critical juncture that the media revived their interest in the project.

Local television stations KUTV and KSL sent out crews to interview Momen and to obtain footage of the construction site near Wendover. A flood of articles and television reports heightened public interest. This publicity also brought with it controversy and heated debate about the artistic merits and appropriateness of the project as a public structure. Due to the technical difficulties with the steel reinforcing of the structure, Momen moved the completion date of the Tree from June to October 1984. He had already sent invitations to numerous civic and national dignitaries, including President Reagan who graciously declined the invitation but nevertheless sent a message wishing Momen great success with the project.

At the height of this intense media focus, Momen received news that would cause his blood to run cold. The soil tests had indicated that his desert site was wholly unsuited to supporting the weight of the finished concrete structure. Whereas original plans had indicated a modest concrete platform at the base of the structure, new cal-

Top right : *24 lengths of steel pipe, each 12 inches in diameter and 90 feet long, were pounded into the desert and then filled with reinforced concrete.*

Below: *A reinforced concrete collar was poured around the piles to lock them in place to create a solid bed for the base of the Tree.*

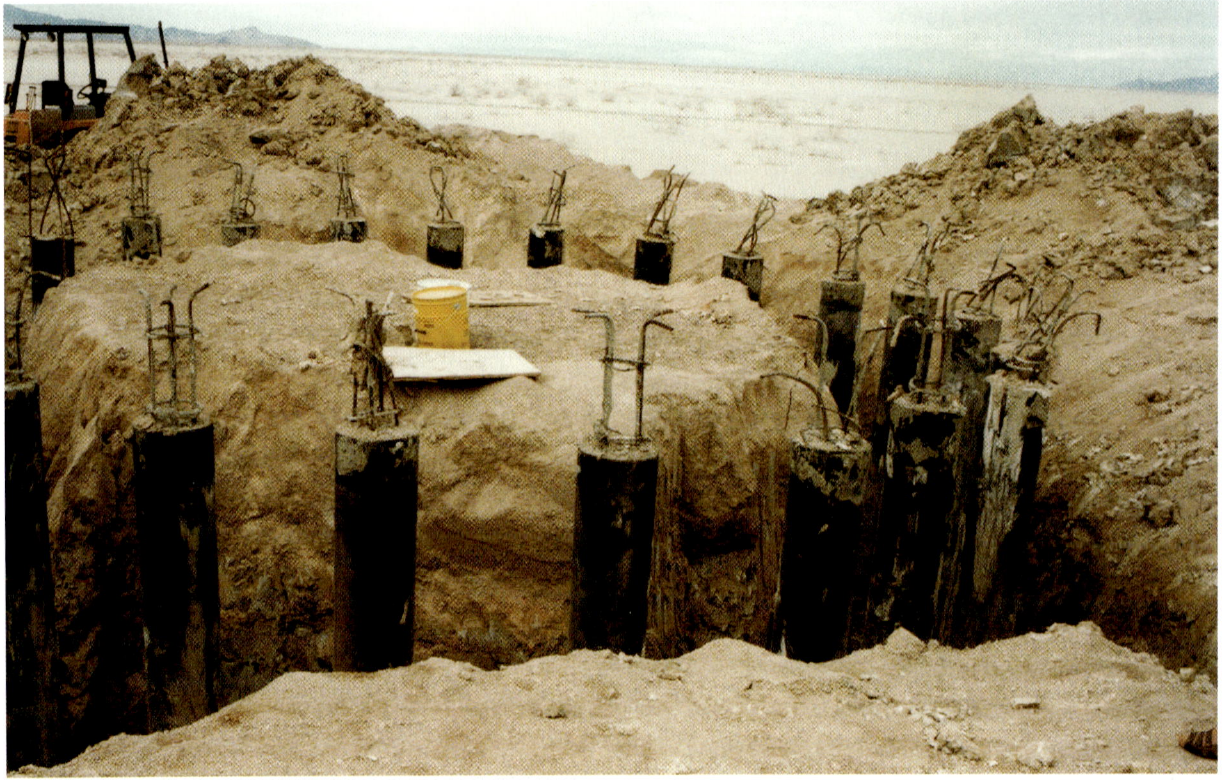

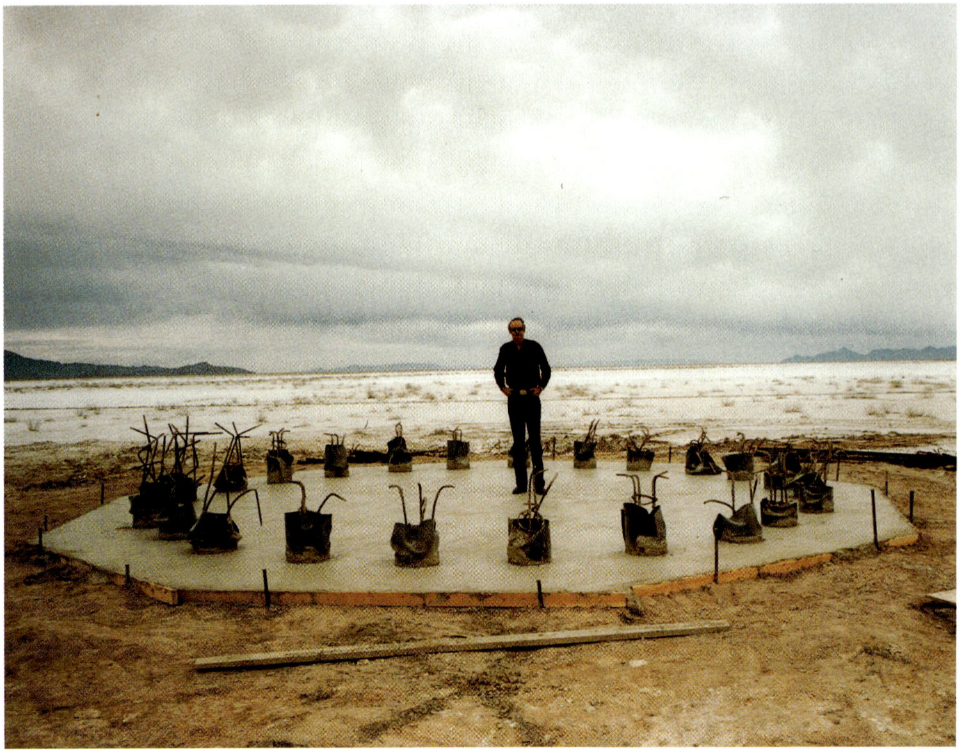

Overleaf: Don Reimann speaks to his son as preparations are made to pour concrete into the matrix of steel bars that has been constructed to reinforce the base of the Tree.

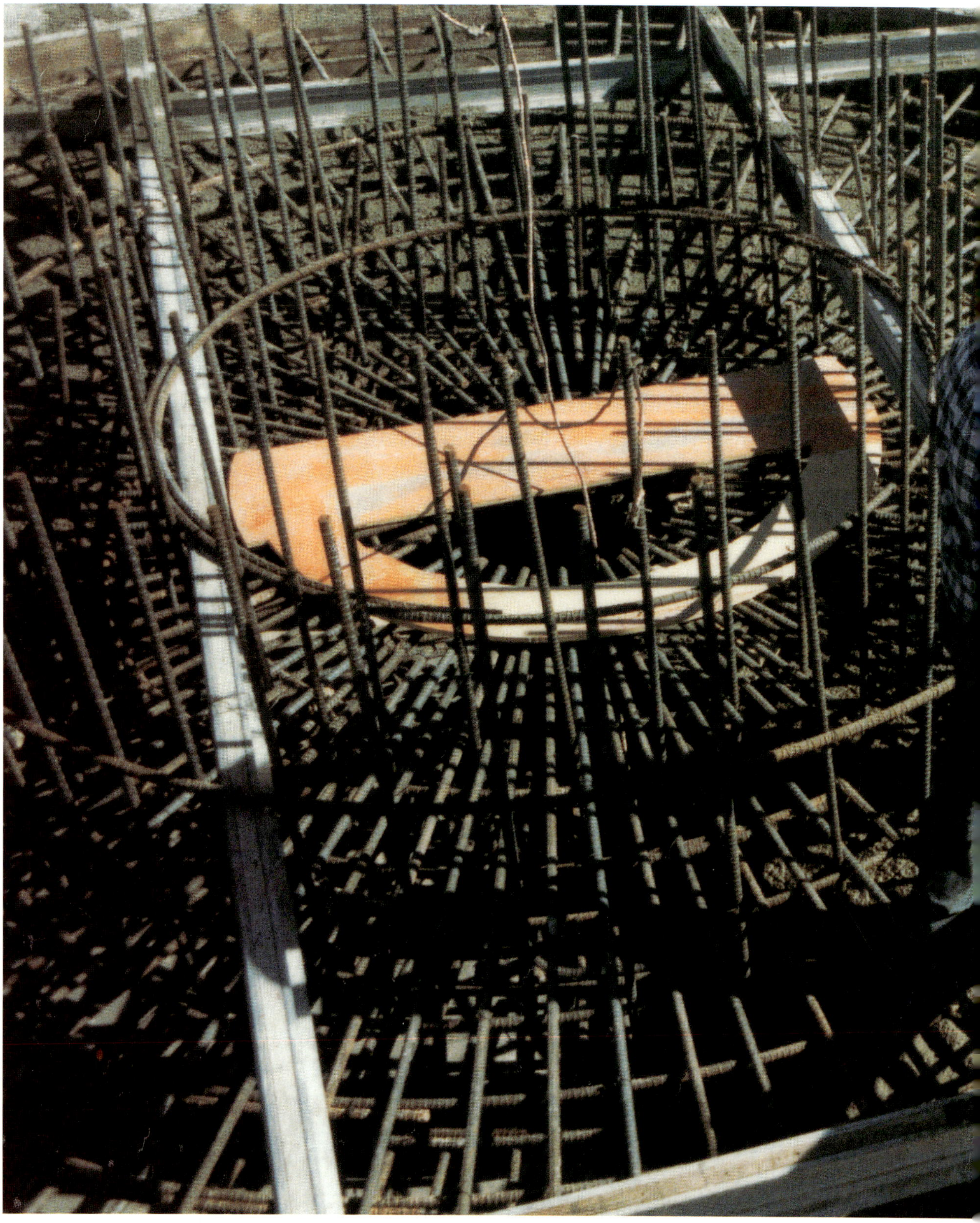

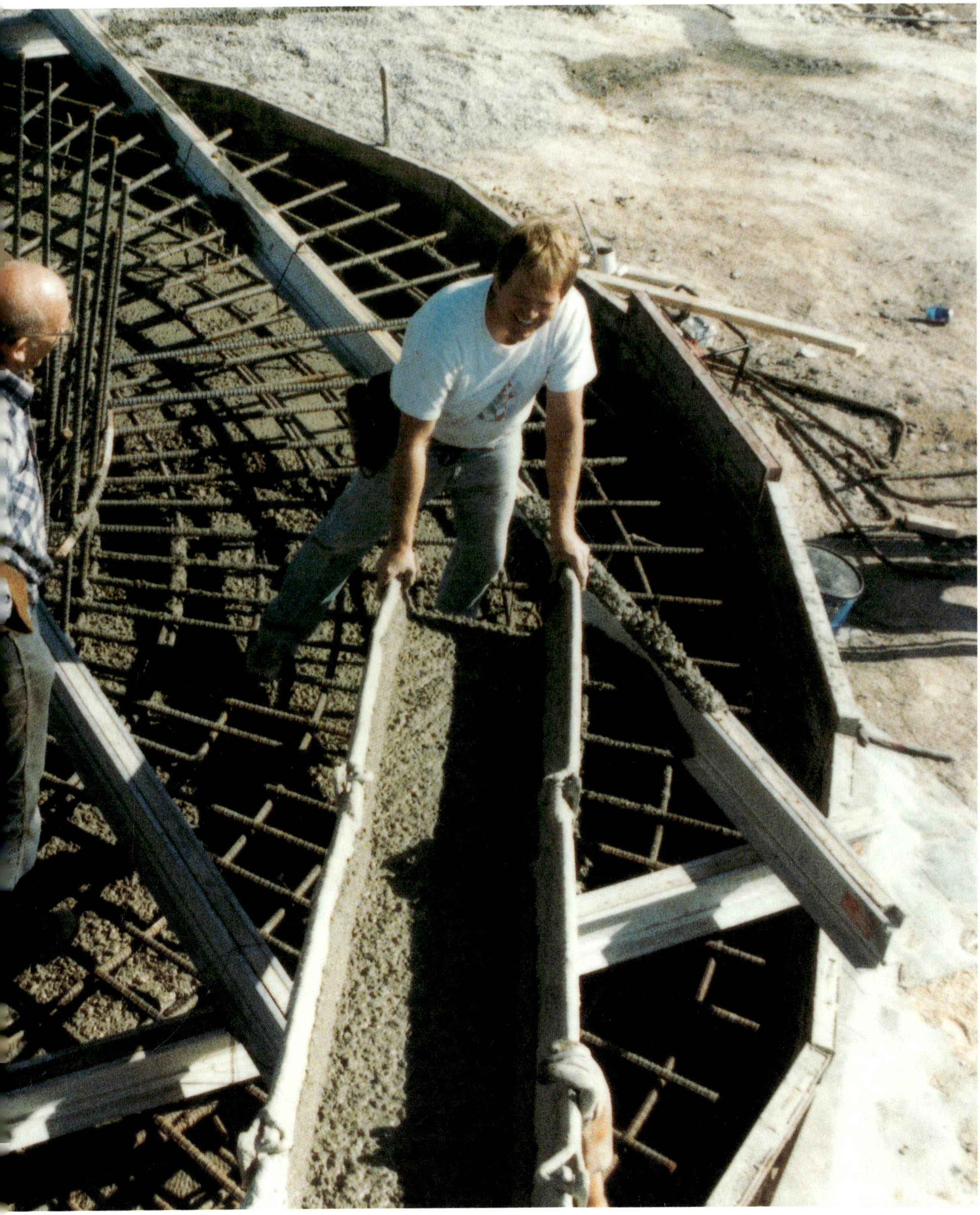

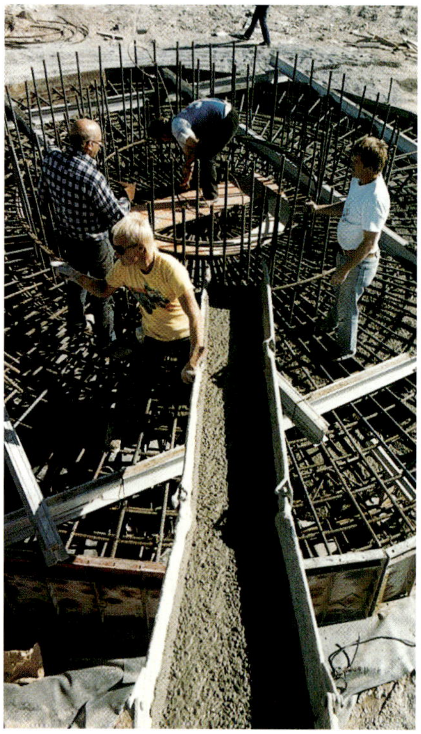

Concrete was hauled from Salt Lake and then poured into the circular shuttering surrounding the reinforcing bars that would form the Tree's foundation slab.

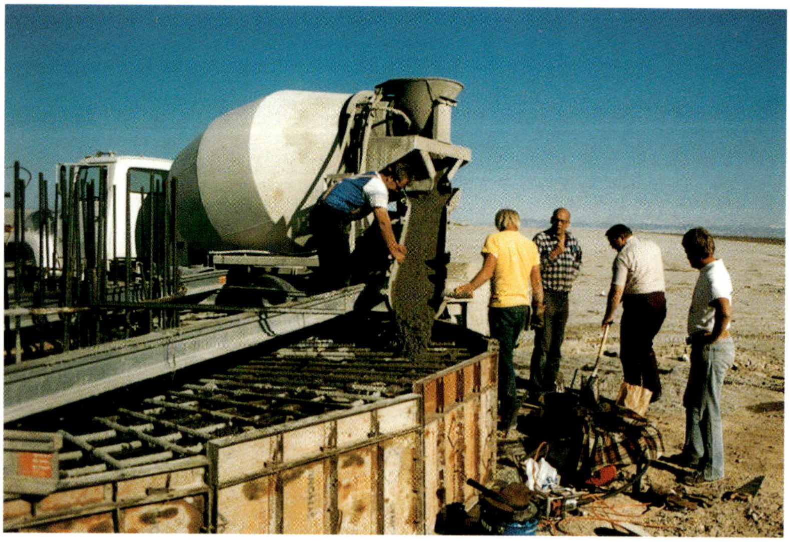

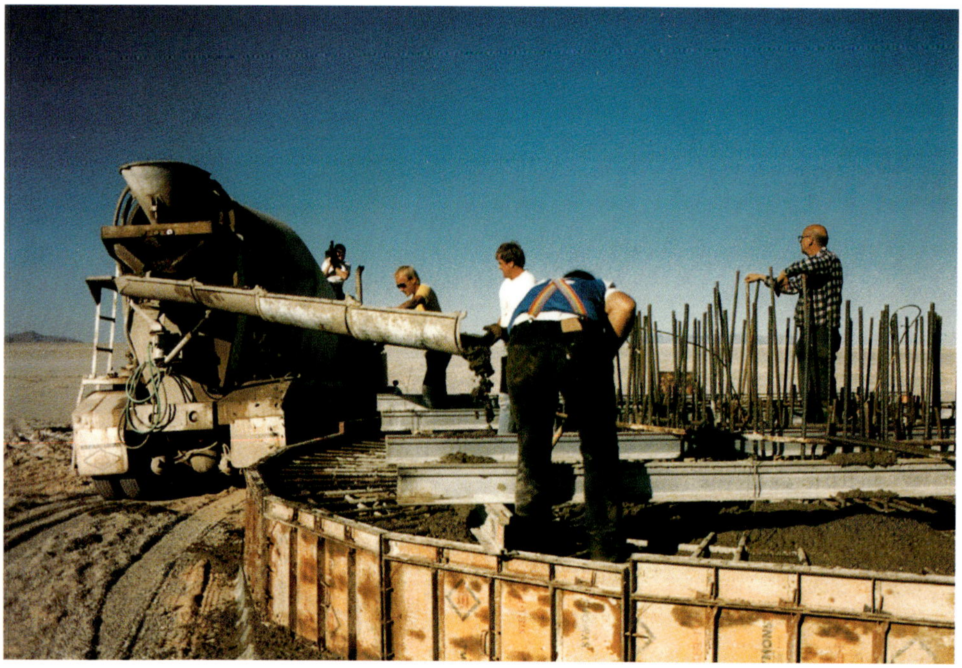

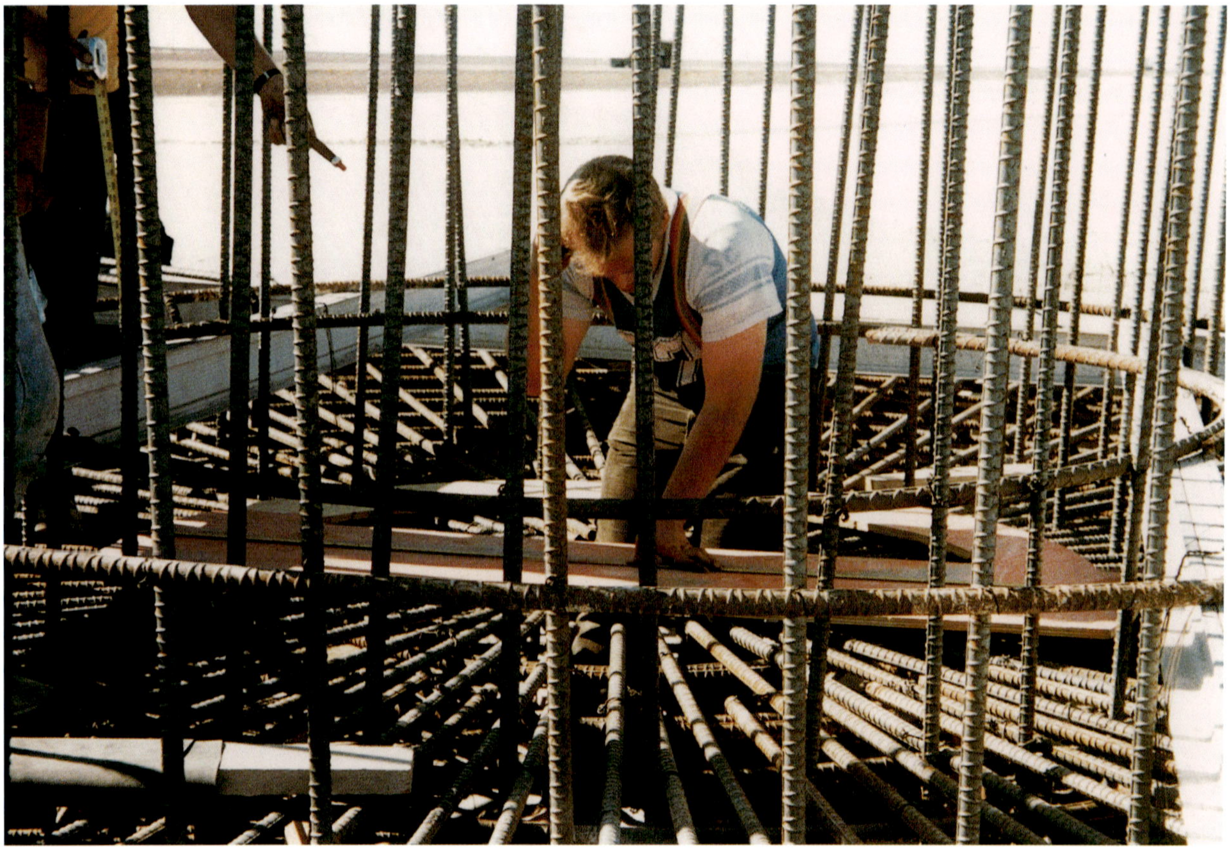

One of Don Reimann's team works on the reinforcing bars that form the girdle that will secure the base of the Tree.

culations called for a vastly modified foundation that would reach deep into the ground. In fact, a ninety- foot deep foundation comprised of twenty-four reinforced concrete piles of one-foot diameter, supporting an eight-foot thick concrete foundation, was now called for! This was an unexpected and totally new ball game for Momen who had thought that he had the end of the project in sight. This new revelation would result in a delay of least six months and more than double the cost of the project. Shocked and dismayed, Momen weighed the options before him.

He could possibly re-design the Tree, reducing the size and mass of its main trunk, its branches, and the spheres. Thoughts of canceling the project crossed his mind. If he did cancel the project this action would give the lie to all his detractors and to the increasingly vociferous opponents of the project. However, if he pressed on, how would he be able to pay for the additional costs? Momen took a few days off to ponder his predicament and finally decided that there was no going back or opting out of the project to which he had committed himself, his friends, and associates. The work would go on and the Tree would be completed as planned. He decided to sell the condominiums he had bought a couple of years previously in Washington D.C. He also sold his cabin in

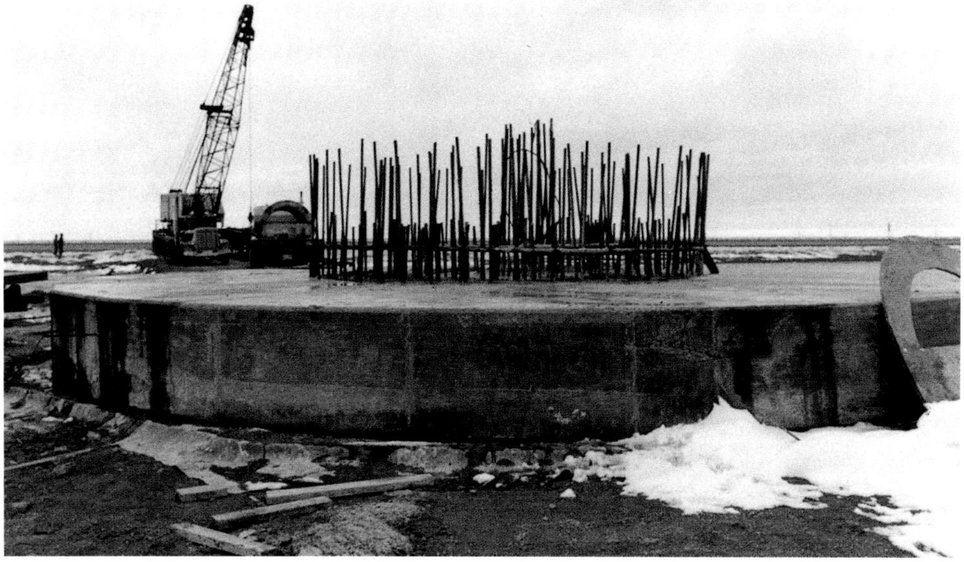

The massive base is revealed after the shuttering has been removed.

northern Sweden and some prize picccs of his personal art collection. With the funds he raised in liquidating these assets, Momen instructed the construction team to go ahead with the original specifications and to include the additional reinforcing to the base and the foundation.

Khosrow Semnani had been coordinating the purchase of materials from numerous suppliers. However, due to the increased work load and the escalating scale of the project he asked Momen to take over as he could no longer cope with his own demanding business interests as well as function as project manager for Momen's enterprise. Word about Momen's unexpected obstacles and financial shortfalls soon got around and suddenly suppliers refused to deliver materials on account. Some suppliers demanded prepayment before even considering an order for this project. However the situation returned to normal when additional funds from the sale of his properties became available and he set about ordering the heavy steel pipes for the foundation piles. The pipe was supplied in thirty foot lengths and three sections had to be welded together to make up the full length of each pile. Before they could be driven into the desert, each pipe had to be sand blasted and treated for corrosion in the hostile saline environment of the desert. Because of the excessive length of the piles it was difficult to find a contractor who was equipped to drive the pipes into the ground. A large crane had to be brought in from out of state by Acme Crane. Because of the unknown conditions of the earth deep below the construction site, Momen could not get a fixed cost estimate for the work from the pile driving company. He decided to proceed on blind faith. It turned out that the piles sank easily and quickly through the first thirty feet as they were pounded through the soft, residue of the prehistoric lake bed that once covered this region, before it drew back to the Pacific Ocean. The pile driving took less time than the contractor had estimated and, thankfully, each pile was firmly bedded in the substrata, thereby providing excellent stability for the foundation slab that would support the Tree, high above the desert floor. After the enormous piles had been driven into the earth, reinforcing steel was lowered down inside the pipes and then each pile was filled with concrete. This operation occupied Don Reimann and his sons for three continuous weeks. By the end of that fall they had also poured the massive concrete foundation base.

Momen had successfully met the financial challenge presented by the unique demands of getting his project underway and, for the moment, he could breathe a sigh of relief. Moreover the contractors had proved their worth in overcoming the extraordinary technical challenges presented by the terrain, and the specific site location. Still more challenges lay ahead. Successful collaboration is an intrinsic aspect of any large project that requires the knowledge, skills and expertise of diverse specialists. All parties to the project would ultimately have to work in complete harmony in order to realize the artist's conception; only in this way would Momen's vision in the desert become a reality. The weather was beginning to turn cold with the onset of winter; icy winds blew unabated across the desolate expanse of the desert. Reimann's crew withdrew from the bleak and inhospitable terrain to the Salt Lake City factory to complete the next phase of their complex undertaking—the forming and casting of the enormous concrete spheres, the largest of which was to measure thirteen-and-a-half feet in diameter and weigh 60 tons.

Chapter five

CONCRETE MOLDS AND SUMMERSAULTS

Reimann knew that there were six different sized spheres to be made and this would require six molds of varying dimensions. The molds were made in quarter segments. Four cast quarter segments would then be welded together to form one sphere. Reimann had considered making half sections but thought that he would encounter problems in pulling the cast forms out of their hemispherical molds. Rigid molds are difficult to separate from their cast forms at the best of times. Even if the molds were perfectly made, the cast hemispherical sections would be very difficult to pull out of their corresponding concave molds. Atmospheric pressure would ensure that the cast forms remained tightly secured within their molds; massive amounts of pulling power would be required to separate them, and the risk of fracturing the cast or damaging the mold was very high.

Reimann settled for quarter-sections as he felt confident that they would strip much easier from their molds without the risk of breakage. The quarter-section molds were made by first pouring two flat slabs of reinforced concrete with corresponding metal inserts. One slab was laid flat on the floor while the other was butted up to it in an upright position. The perpendicular slab was then welded to the horizontal slab along their metal inserts to form an exact corner section. The precise measurement of this right angle was critical to the success of the casting; any inaccuracy at this point would be magnified throughout the casting process. Within the right angle of the two concrete slabs, wooden frames were constructed with curved surfaces bulging outward like giant orange segments. In order to make the frames, wooden strips were bowed over a series of bulkheads, like the hull of a ship, to replicate a quarter section of the surface of each sphere as accurately as possible. These wooden frames would be used to form the convex surfaces from which the concrete molds for the spheres would be made. The

A wooden armature is constructed to support the Plaster-of-Paris that will, in turn, become the former for one of the sphere's quadrant molds.

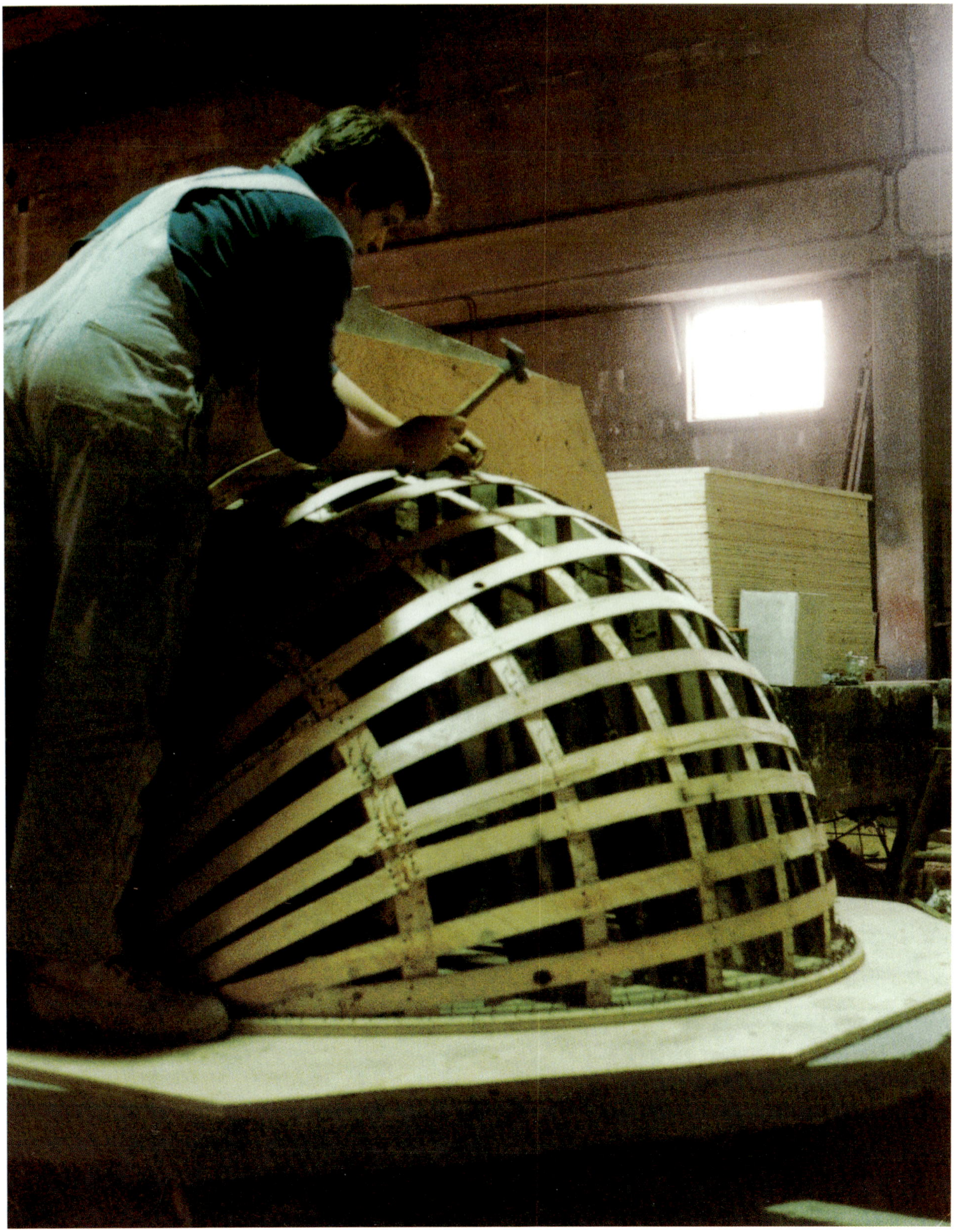

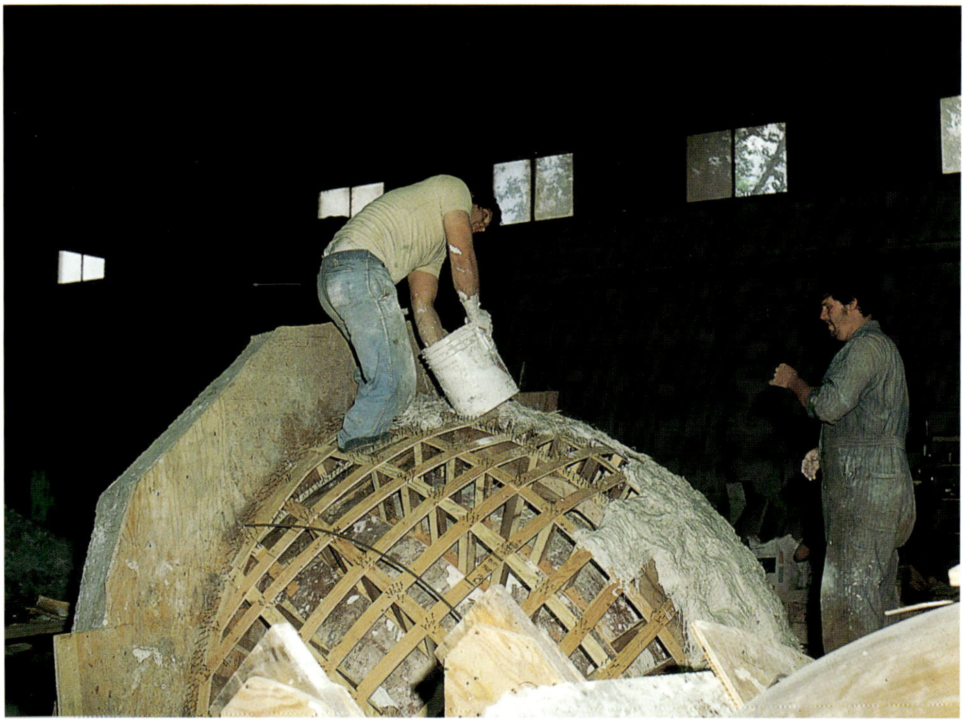

Left: *A worker pours Plaster-of-Paris over the wooden armature.*

Below: *A curved steel bar indicates the circumference profile that the surface of the plaster will conform to.*

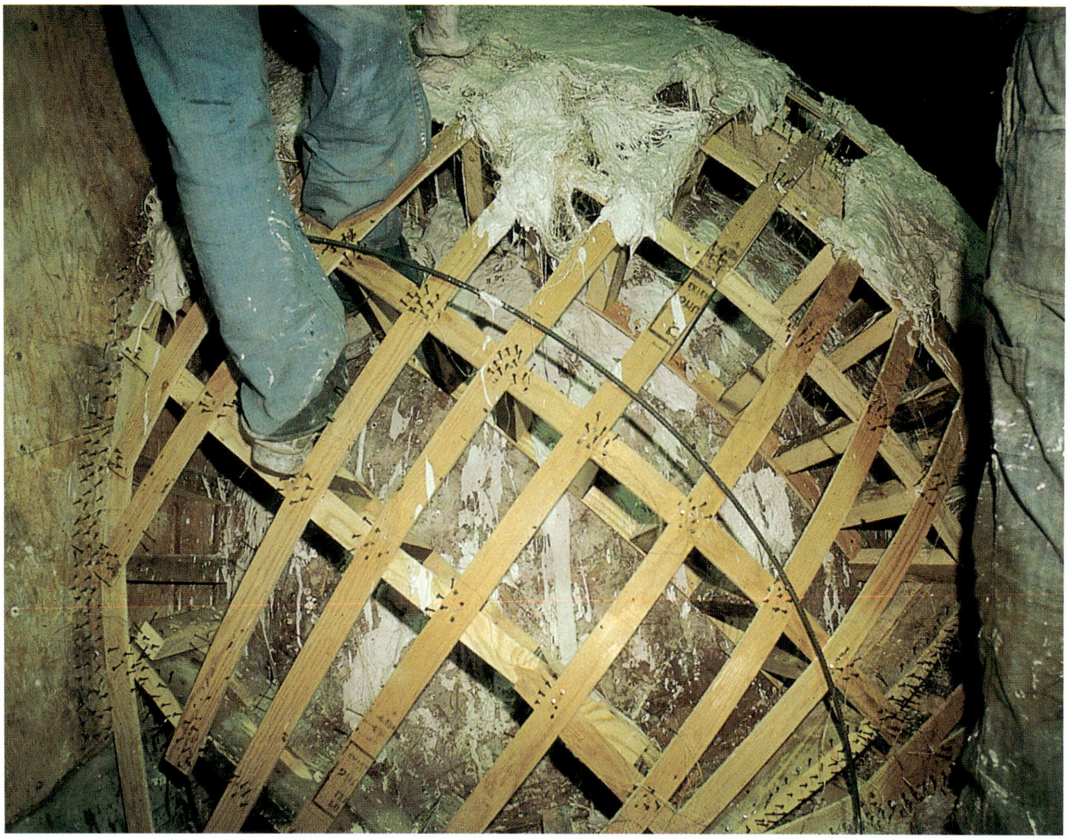

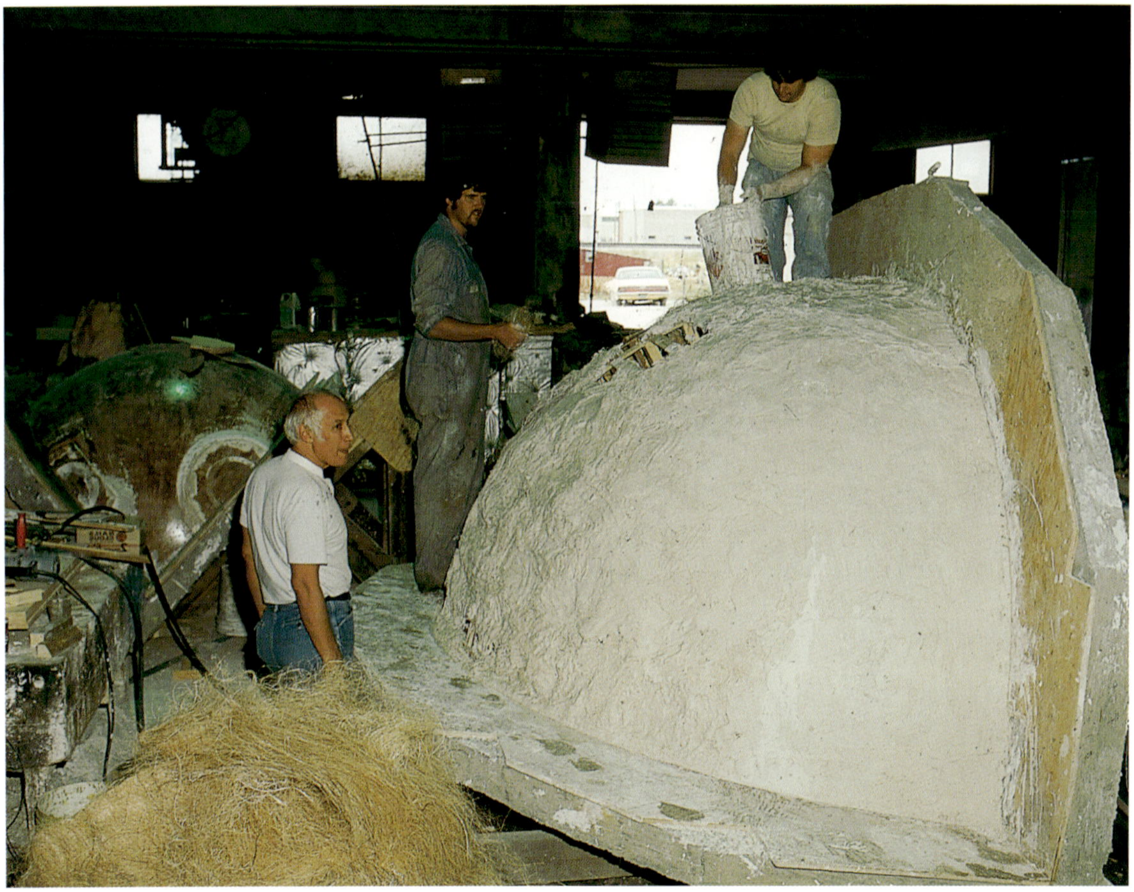

Momen watches as workers cover a wooden armature with plaster.

adjacent concrete slabs would form the "stops" for the concrete casting material in each case.

Wet plaster would have to be applied over the wooden frames to ensure that the surface would end up perfectly spherical. Casting plaster was used, as it is not as hard as other cement materials that would set so hard that they could not easily be shaped. In order to shape the plaster surface of the spheres and to remove high spots, large curved screeds would have to be constructed. These screeds would be rotated over the surface of the plaster to shave off excess material before it set. Each screed was made of heavy wood, to prevent any flexing, and faced with a 1/4 inch thick aluminum plate that was laboriously hand filed by Reimann to conform to the circumference profile of each sphere. The cutting edge of the curved screed had to be as sharp as a knife to cut through the setting plaster as the blade was moved over the spherical frame. The edge of the screed had to be beveled at 10 degrees so that it did not drag and get stuck on the surface. The aluminum screeds were tightly pivoted with steel dowels inserted into the polar axes of each wooden frame, allowing the hemispherical edges of the screeds

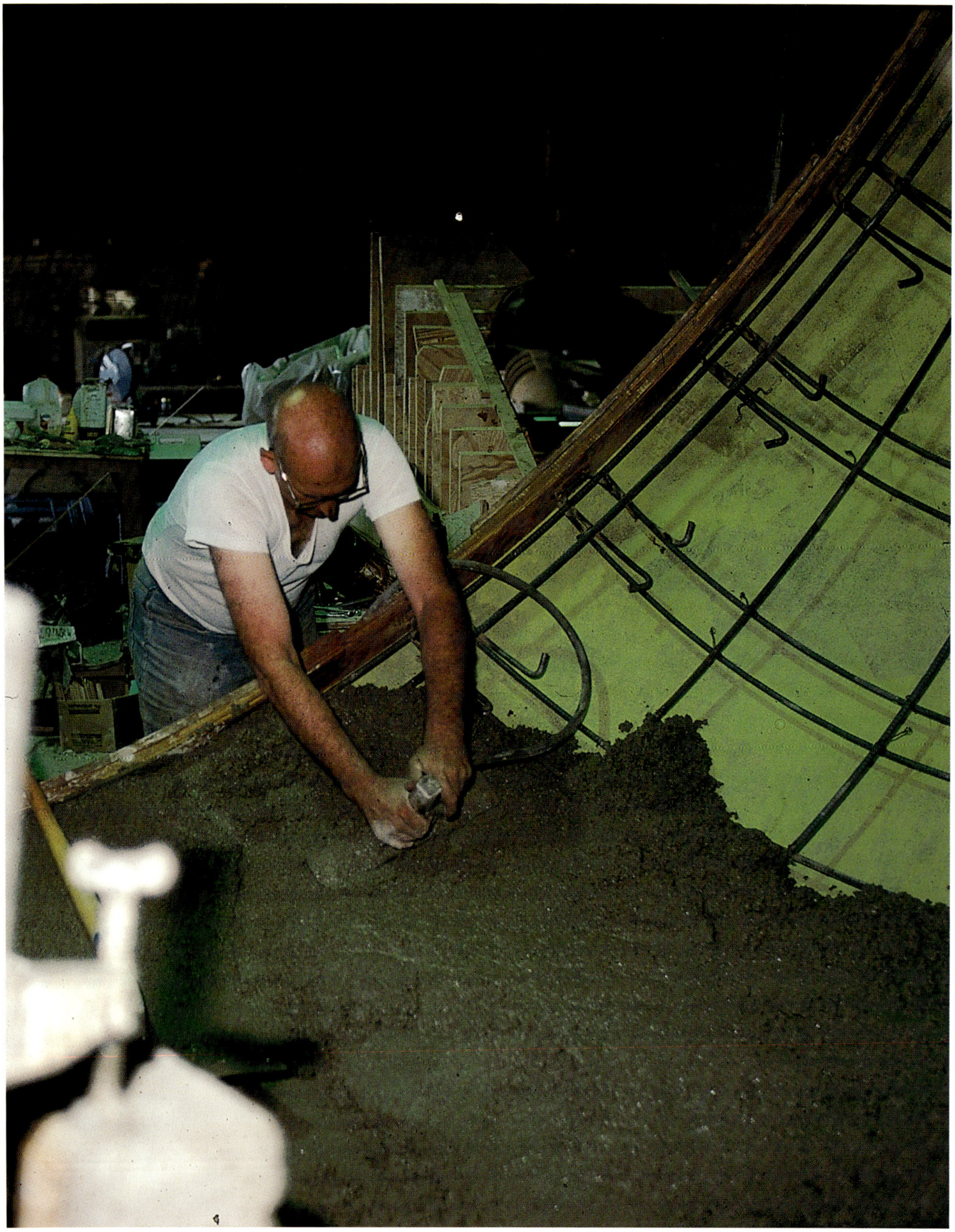

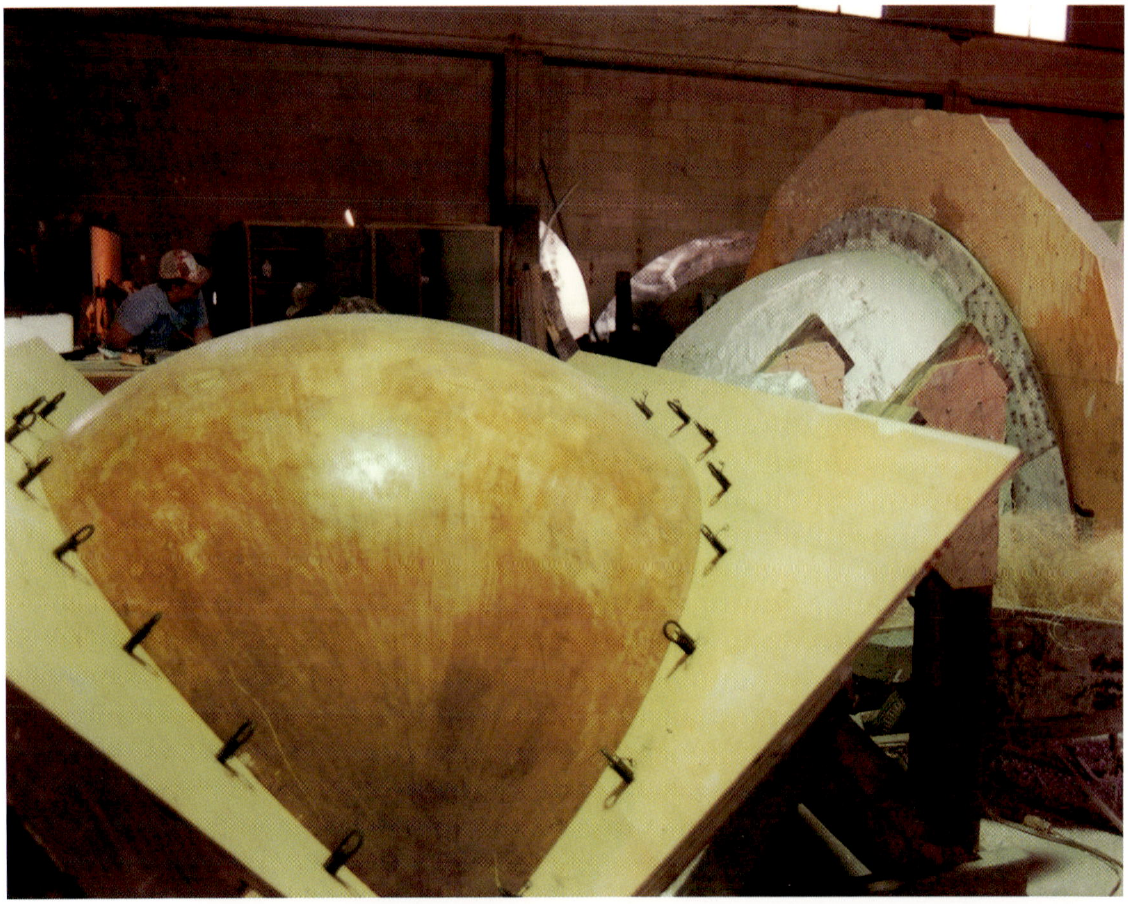

Left: *Concrete is carefully poured into the reinforcing bars of one of the molds to create a sphere quadrant.*

Top: *After the plaster former has set and dried it is painted with Shellac to seal the pores of the material and to allow the concrete mold to release easily.*

Right: *A concrete mold indicating the position of reinforcing bars in preparation for the pouring of one of the sphere quadrants.*

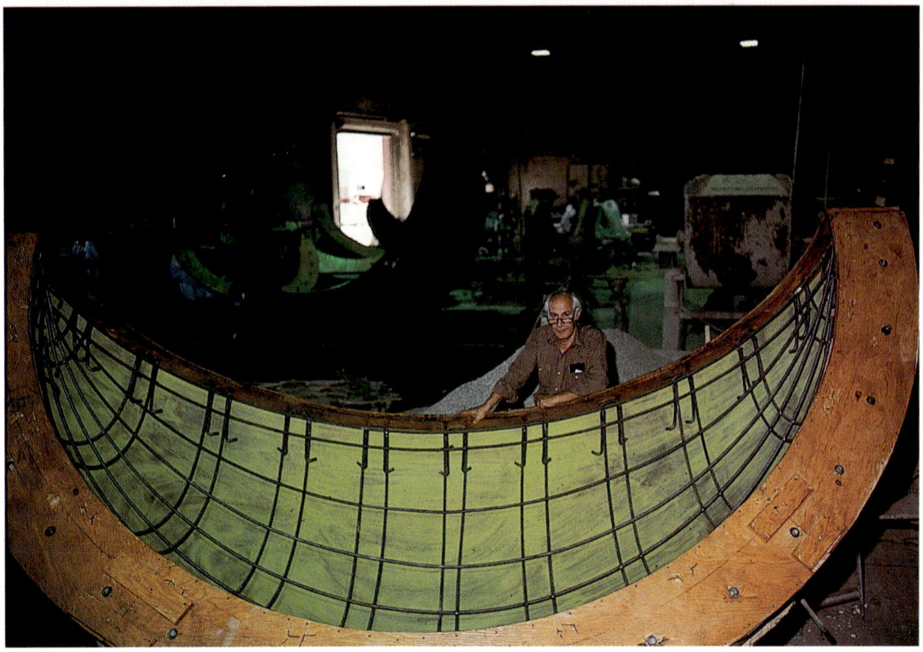

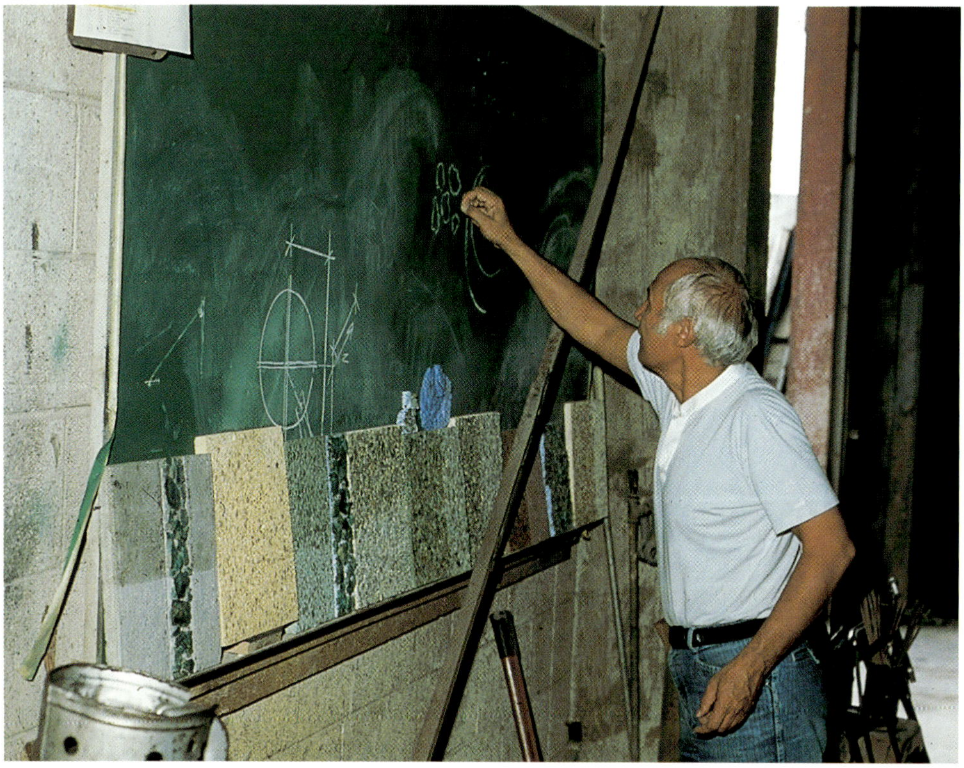

Left: *Karl Momen illustrates a technical point on the chalkboard at Don Reimann's factory.*

Below: *Completed quadrant molds.*

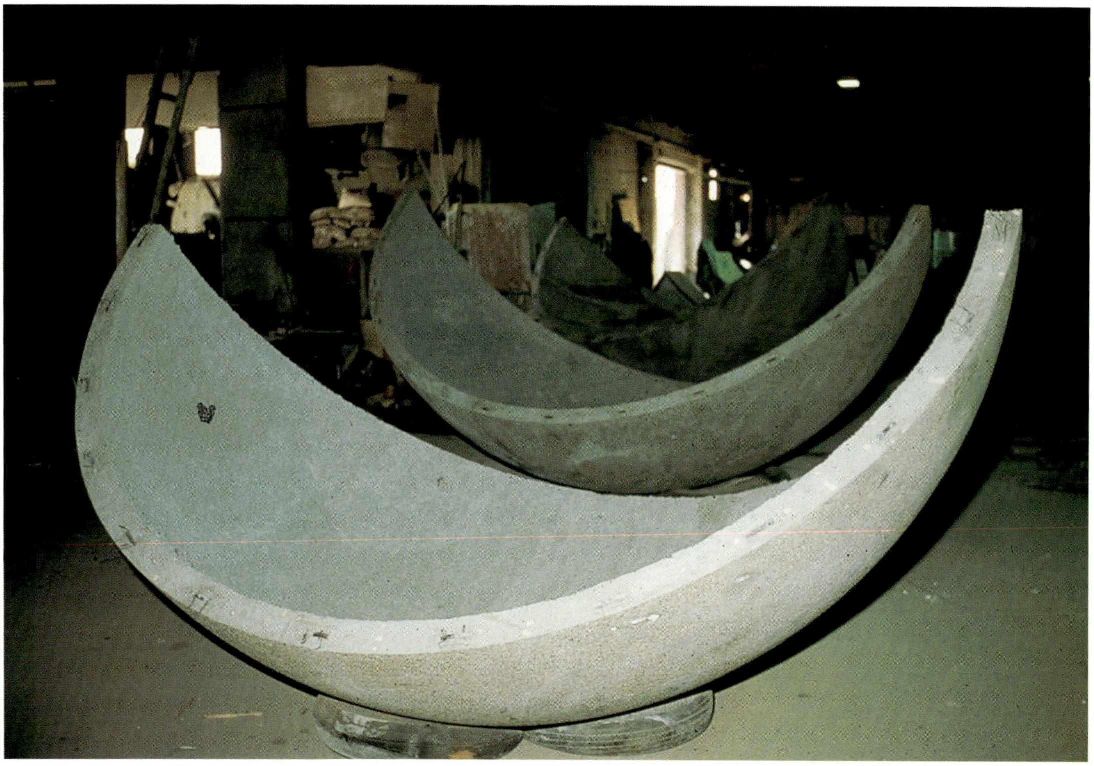

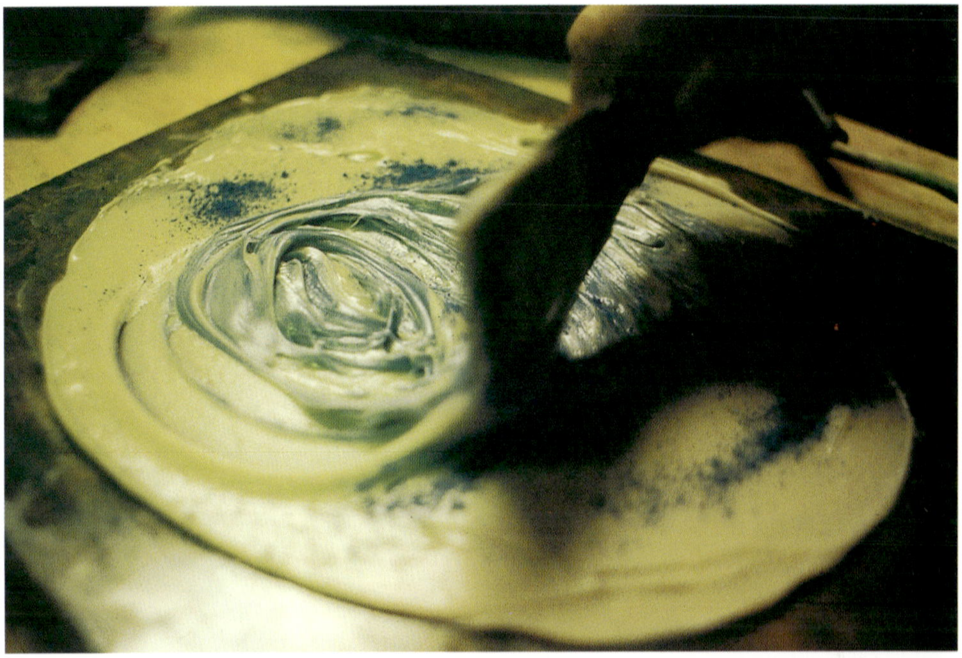

Right: *A worker mixes epoxy adhesive prior to securing chrysocolla rocks to the surface of a sphere.*

Below: *A rock is adhered to the epoxy-coated surface of one of the smaller spheres.*

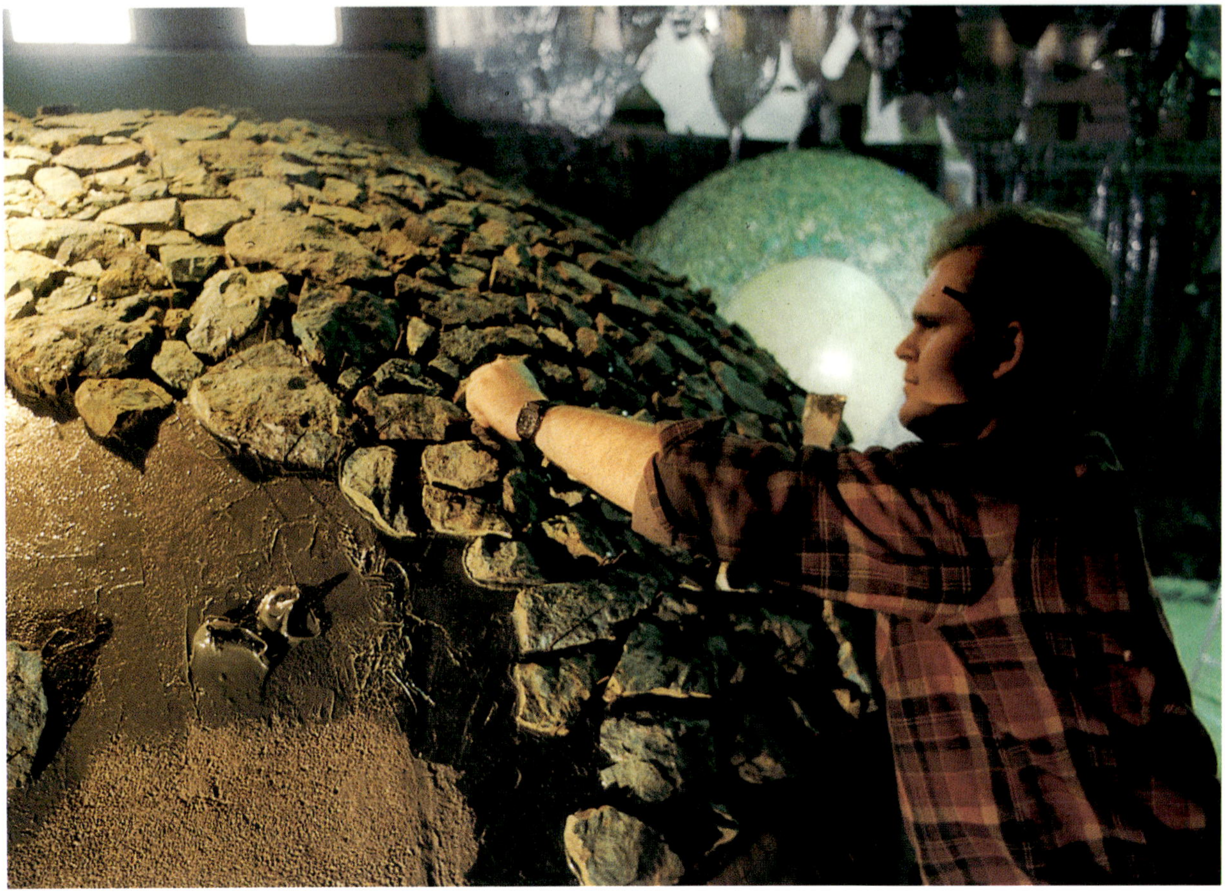

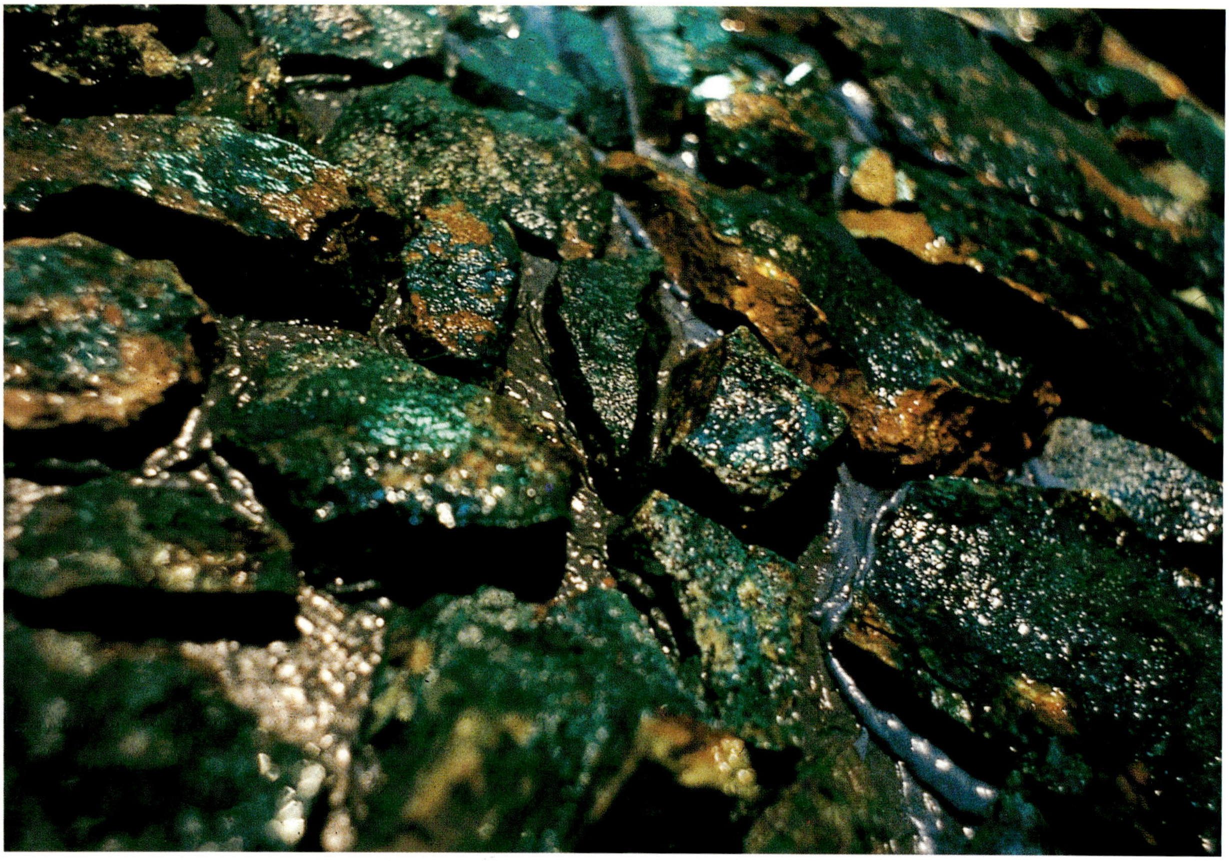

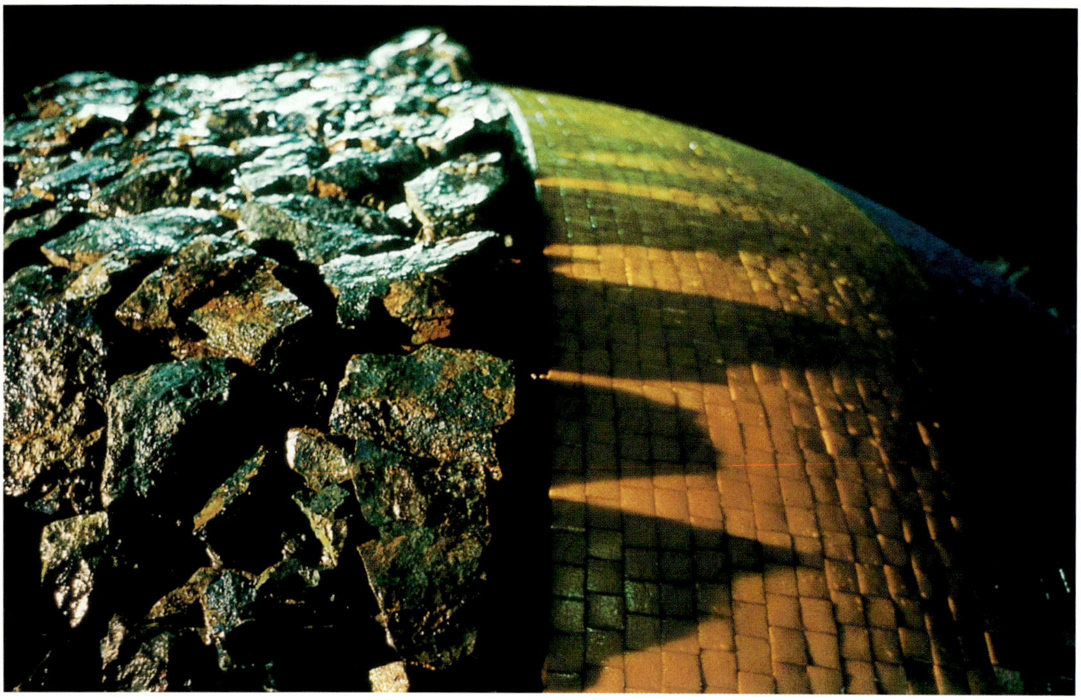

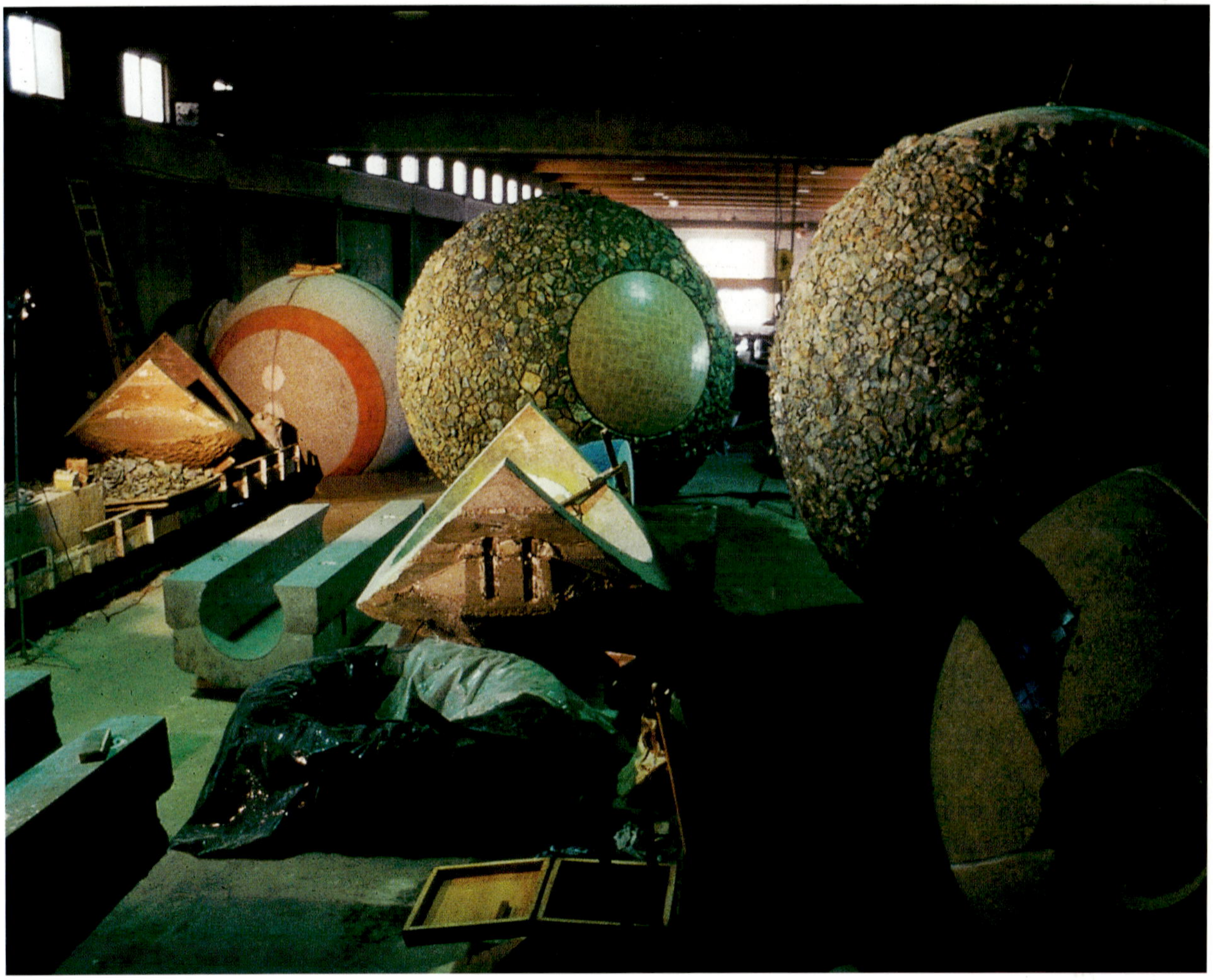

Top: *The completed spheres on the floor of Don Reimann's factory prior to being moved out to the desert.*

Opposite: *Close-up of the rocks adhered to the surface of one of the smaller spheres.*

Overleaf: *Don Reimann washing down one of the spheres with a garden hose.*

to traverse the curved surfaces of the wooden frames. The screeds had to made to exact specifications and pivoted in such a way that they did not move backward or forward, or in and out of their precise alignment with the surfaces of the spheres. Plaster-of-Paris was then carefully mixed in large buckets and carefully applied to the wooden frame. Hemp was mixed into the plaster to contain the sloppy mixture from dropping through the gaps in the planking of the frame and to add reinforcing to the material. As each batch of wet plaster had a limited setting time of approximately 20 minutes, Reimann and his team had to work quickly to screed off the excess material before it set. If they were too slow in this task the plaster would set and lock the screed to the surface, creating an awful mess and hold up the work. The layer of hemp and plaster was applied until it came to within a quarter of an inch of the screed blade to allow for swelling of the plaster as it cured. A final mixture of plaster was then applied to the hardened sur-

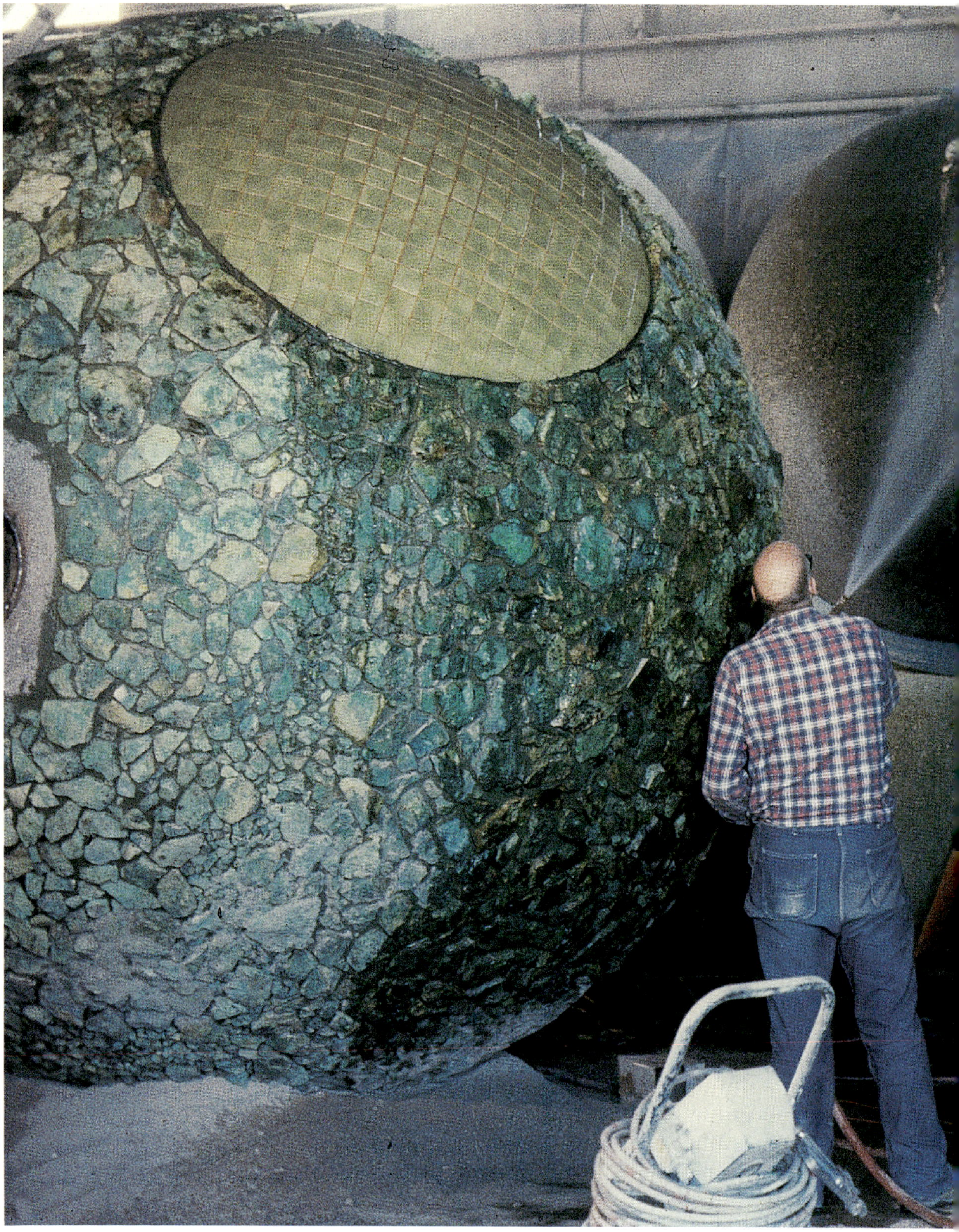

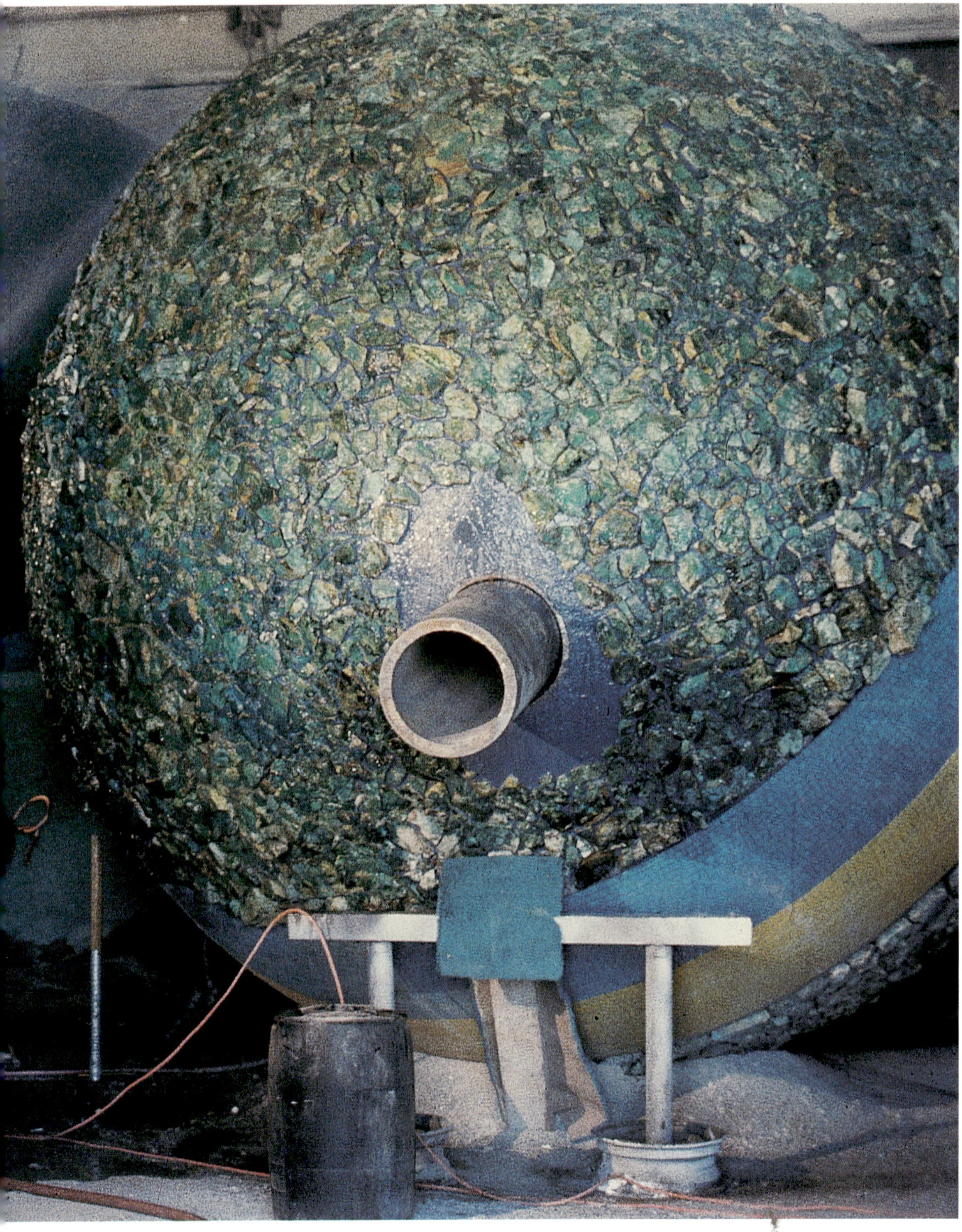

face and the screed was moved backward and forward to carefully trim off high spots as the plaster set.

Once the quadrant sections of the spheres were completed they were allowed to thoroughly dry out for a couple of days and then they were painted with shellac. Three coats of shellac were applied to the surface of each spherical section. The shellac soaked in and sealed the pores of the plaster, creating a smooth non-porous surface. It would be on this smooth surface that the concrete mix for the concave molds would be cast. A waxy compound was applied over the surface of the shellac to ensure an easy release for the concrete and then a matrix of heavy steel reinforcing bars was laid over the curved surface of each segment. An 8-inch thick layer of concrete was then cast and carefully vibrated to release any air bubbles trapped in the mixture. When the molds had cured they were removed with the aid of an overhead crane and carefully laid on their backs. Side plates were placed along the edges to contain the concrete mix. The concave surfaces of the molds were then sealed with epoxy and the waxy form-release was again applied to the concave surfaces to receive the final mix of concrete that would constitute the actual sphere sections. Half-inch thick steel reinforcing rods were again formed and placed over the surface of the concave molds and then the concrete sections of each sphere were cast to a thickness of three-and-a-half inches. The concrete mix was comprised of three parts of "pea" gravel, two parts of sand, and one part of cement. This mix resulted in extremely strong concrete that could withstand a pressure of about four tons per square inch.

It was important to make the spheres hollow, otherwise they would be unmanageably heavy. Steel inserts were cast into the adjacent edges of the quadrants so that four identical sections could be welded together to complete each sphere. Welding the sections of the sphere together was a difficult and risky task. All the welding had to be done from the inside of each hollow sphere. The only access to each sphere was a small round hole, barely big enough for a man to wiggle his body through. The risks of claustrophobia and inhaling toxic welding fumes was high. These holes would later serve to anchor the spheres to the concrete "branches" of the Tree, high above the desert. Once inside the spheres it was difficult to climb out. On one occasion John had to be pulled out with a line dropped to him from the overhead crane. This incident resulted in John loosing his trousers as the rough edges of the concrete ripped the clothing from his body as he was lifted out of the sphere

The trunk of the Tree was cast in similar fashion to the spheres. A tubular model was constructed from wood and covered in plaster. As the plaster was setting, a special screed was pushed along its length to establish the correct profile for the trunk. On one occasion two of Reimann's sons were both pushing the screed along the thirty-six foot section with a freshly poured layer of plaster. This particular mix was beginning to

Opposite: *Momen poses in between two of the completed spheres indicating their relative scale.*

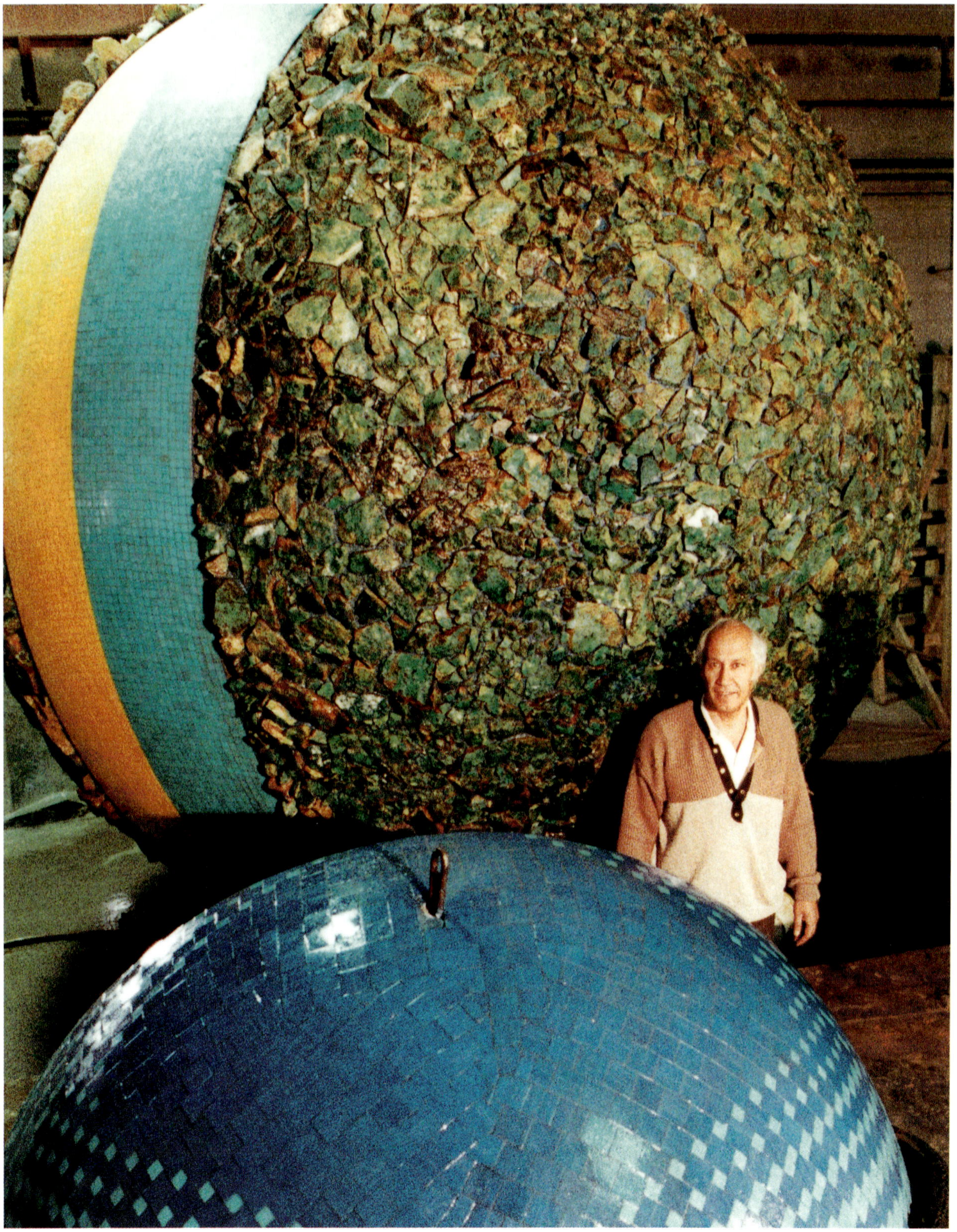

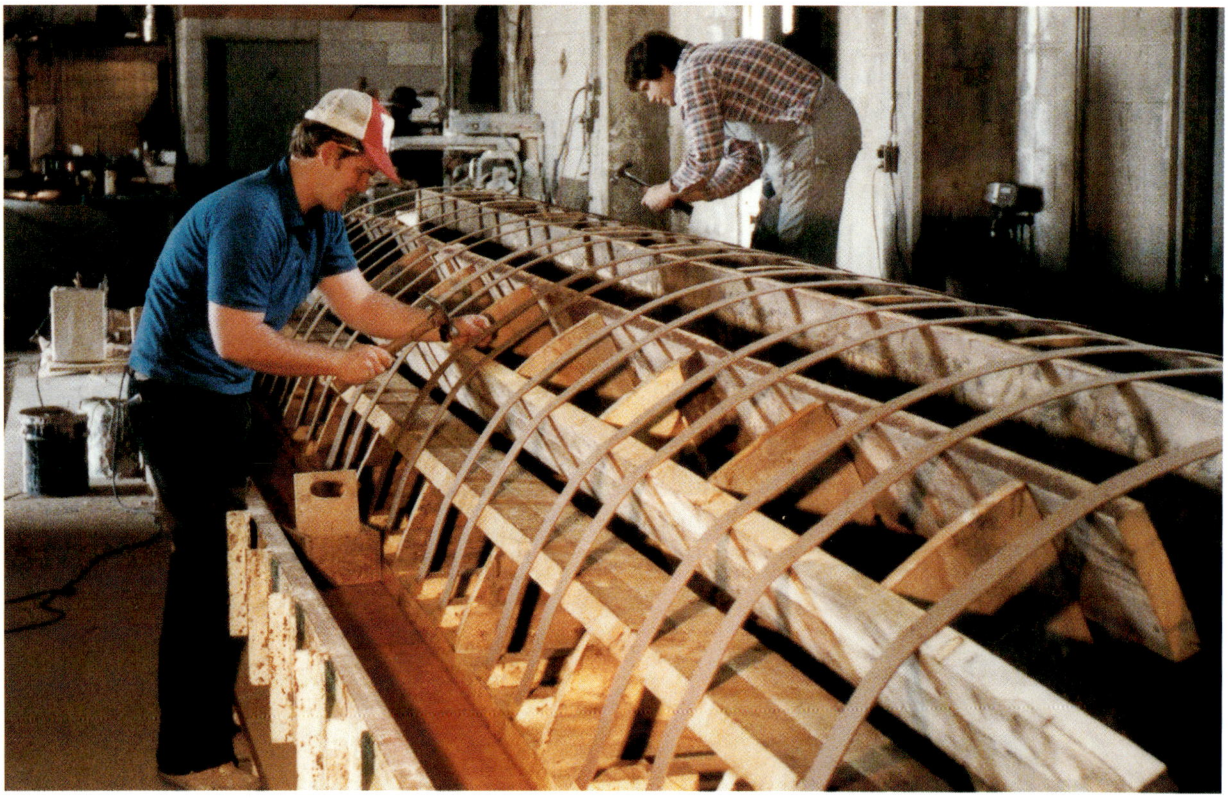

Making the armature for a section of the Tree's "trunk."

set rather rapidly. Fearing that the screed would get hopelessly bogged down in the setting plaster, they decided to take a run at it. So, with both young men pushing for all they were worth they accelerated down the length of the model. It was at this moment that the chemistry of the plaster took over, and the screed came to an instantaneous stop. Both men were somersaulted through the air, landing on their backs on the floor of their father's factory—much to the amusement of the other workers.

When the full-scale model was finally screeded to its final dimensions, concrete mold sections were cast from its surfaces. The final Tree trunk was then cast as six longitudinal sections that were welded and bolted together. The surfaces of the four smaller spheres where cast with a retarding process that resulted in the quartz aggregate of the concrete mix being exposed on the surface. This rough finish was compatible with the texture that Momen had specified for these smaller spheres. However, the two largest spheres were to receive the cut rock that the Reimanns had quarried in southern Utah. It now became important to determine how the color striations on the large spheres were to be accomplished. There were no natural materials available locally that matched the colors called for by Momen's design. After some deliberation Momen decided to import the finest quality ceramic tile from Italy, at considerable personal expense. Because of

Right: *The wooden armature being coated with a layer of Plaster-of-Paris.*

Below: *John Reimann is seen next to the partially completed former that will be used to make a mold for the "trunk" of the Tree.*

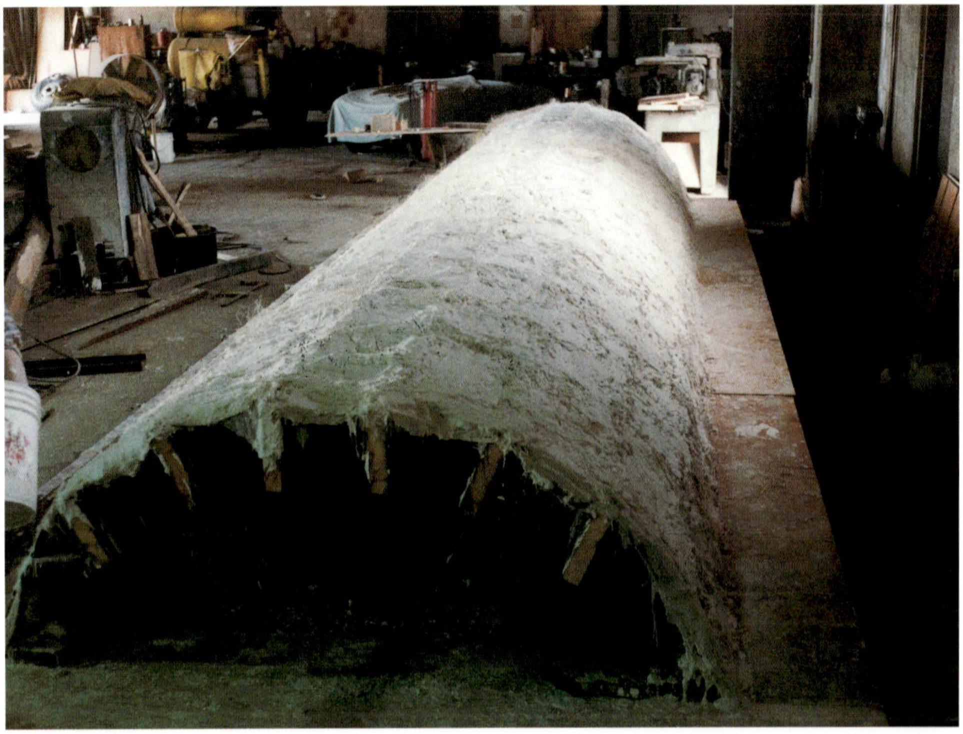

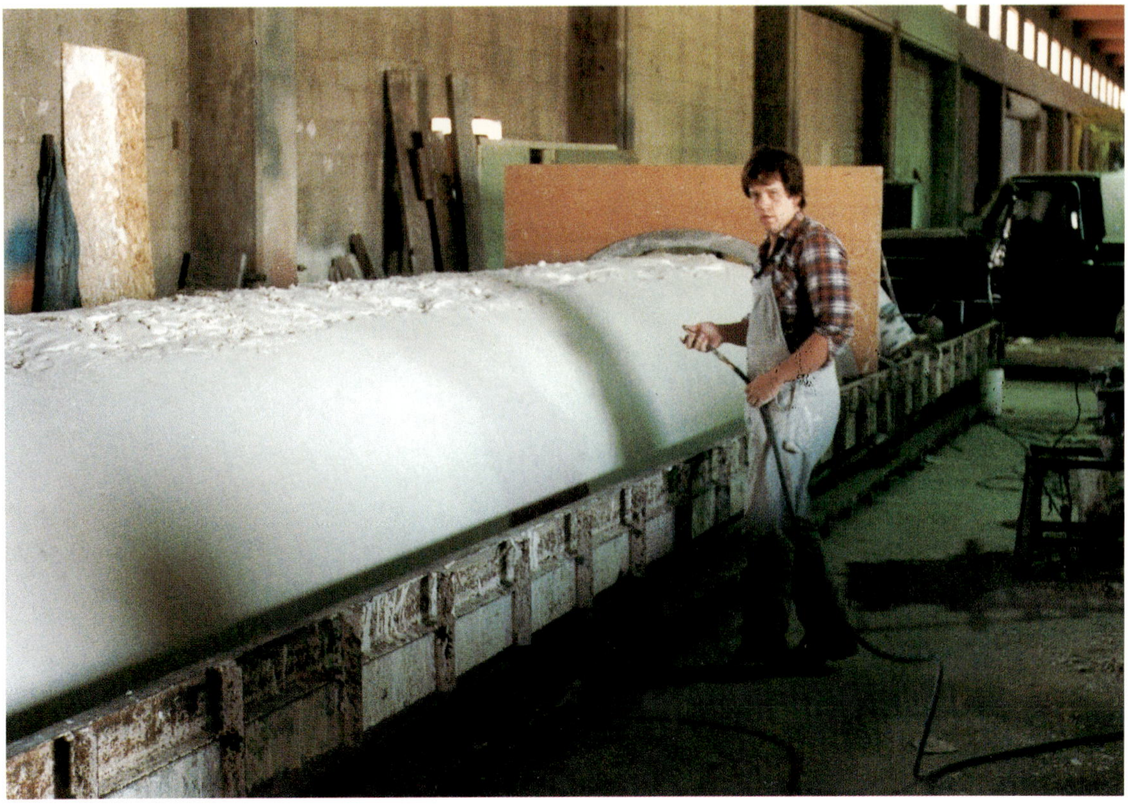

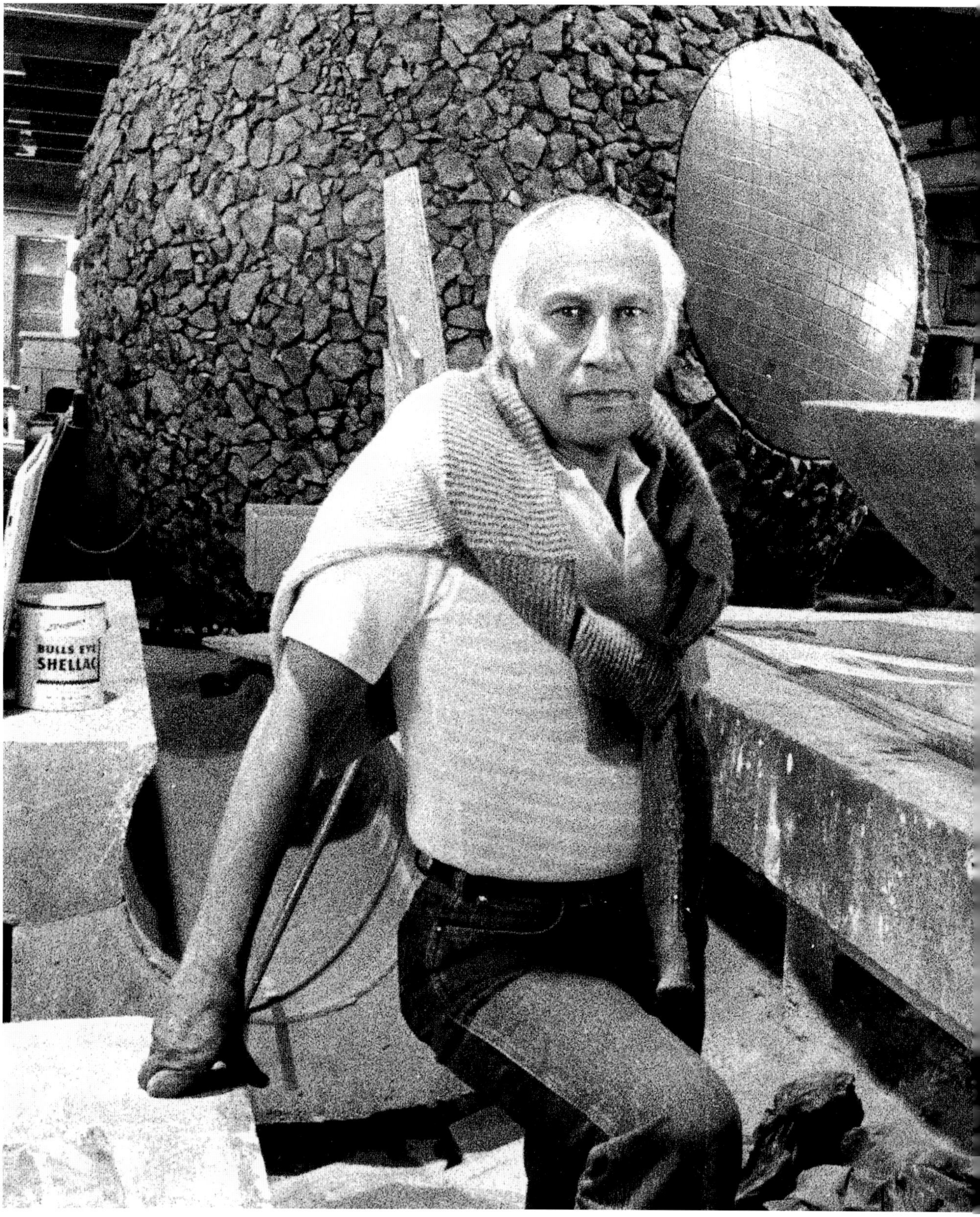
BULLS EYE
SHELLAC

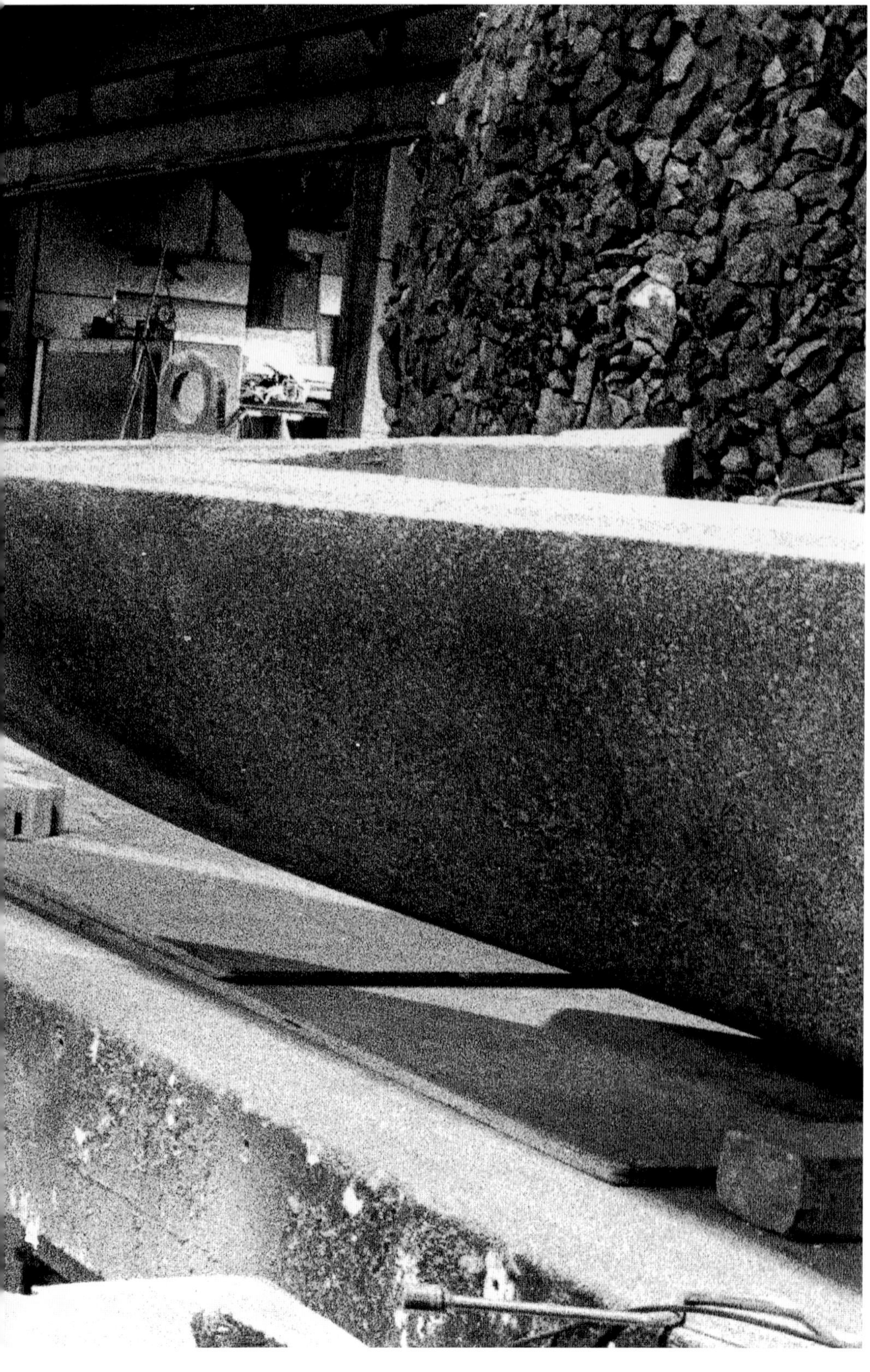

Momen in Don Reimann's factory durig the casting of the spheres.

the scarcity of this high quality tile, the order had to be pre-paid before it was shipped. The best means to attach the tile material to the concrete spheres had also to be determined. After investigation by Reimann, a special brand of epoxy was identified as the most suitable adhesive. It also turned out to be the most expensive product of its kind. The epoxy had to be colored with pigment to a rich blue to harmonize with the natural color of the blue-green stone, before it could be applied.

During the winter months of 1985, Reimann and his workers occupied themselves with gluing first, ceramic tiles, and then the blue and green crystalline rock, piece by piece, to cover the surfaces of each of the larger concrete spheres. In order to rotate the large spheres without damage to their surfaces, and to prevent the spheres from rolling uncontrollably around the floor of Reimann's factory,they were placed on a thick bed of building sand. The spheres could then be carefully rotated so that new rock could be cemented onto their uppermost surfaces as they were rolled over the sand. Colored ceramic tile was cemented directly onto the concrete surfaces of the spheres to form the colorful equatorial bands that circumscribe the largest spheres. In accordance with Momen's design, two of the smaller spheres were then welded together like two soap-bubbles adhering to each other, to make a double sphere.

Momen and Reimann were optimistic that the project would soon be accomplished. Technical challenges had been met and overcome; the end was in sight. The successful completion of all of the components of the structure had nearly been accomplished. Things had been moving ahead quite smoothly—perhaps too smoothly for Momen's ill-fated stars. The cash reserves that Momen had tried to husband in order to see the project to completion had been running dangerously low. Once again the prospect of economic failure loomed large on the horizon. Momen would have no alternative but to call a halt to the operation as he could no longer finance the daily running expenses of the operation. He would not be able to keep Reimann and his team working on the project. This blow was all the more bitter to accept as Momen and his team were within striking distance of realizing the fruit of their labors.

Chapter six

THE HIGH PRICE OF SUCCESS

Just as Reimann can be credited with great innovative powers in meeting the technical challenges of the construction of the Tree, so Momen displayed great tenacity and creativity in the face of crushing financial pressures. Few artists have had unlimited resources to meet the financial costs of their creative imaginations. As the project developed Momen had refused to make compromises of scale or quality of materials and consequently had to cope with the financial implications. As his own funds were exhausted he was compelled to seek various loans. A loan raised in Sweden was not enough and swallowing his pride he turned to his local artist friends, Dennis Smith and Gary Smith. Out of a genuine desire to help a dedicated and struggling fellow artist, they agreed to co-sign for a $30,000 loan from Copper State Savings and Loan Company for Momen.

The project lurched precariously forward, but with escalating expenses, this money was quickly exhausted, and Momen was forced to turn to his good friend Kosroh Semnani for yet another loan of $150,000. The end was not yet in sight and by August these funds had also been spent. At this late stage in the project Momen had no other alternative but to call a halt to the operation and Reimann called his team off the job. Work came to a stop and Reimann grudgingly moved on to other contracts to maintain his own viability. Eventually Momen was compelled to turn to his long-time friend, Bertil Jonsson, the proprietor of Art and Form, an art dealership in Stockholm. Jonsson magnanimously provided two successive loans of $30,000 and $50,000, saving the operation from failure. Jonsson had to wire money to Momen to pre-pay Acme Crane company. The company had refused to move their large crane from Oregon to Salt Lake City for the final erection, until they had received payment. Part of these loans would also be used to finance the costs of the dedication ceremony. Momen was able to recall

Reimann's team and preparation for the erection of the Tree resumed. The project was now very near to completion, all the components of the Tree had been completed and were ready for final assembly.

The completed spheres and the trunk sections were loaded onto flatbed trucks, ready to be transported to the construction site in the desert. It was while the enormous double sphere was being loaded onto the bed of the truck that the sling of the twenty-ton crane broke, bringing its precious load crashing to the ground. Miraculously, no damage was incurred, and after careful inspection, the concrete spheres were found to be completely unscathed. Reimann believed that this was the unscheduled test that proved the quality of his team's engineering abilities. Once loaded, the convoy moved onto the Interstate 80 highway towards the remote construction site.

Momen had found it practically impossible to find an insurance company that was prepared to insure the components of his giant sculpture while in transit to the construction site, at a reasonable rate. The insurance companies' valuations of the concrete spheres resulted in astronomical figures, with the result that the premiums that they asked were far more than Momen could possibly have afforded at the time. Consequently the seventy-five mile road trip was undertaken entirely at Momen's personal risk. Fortunately for all concerned, the convoy of vehicles arrived safely at the construction site without any further mishaps. Reimann employed the finest welder he could find to assist his son, Gary, in welding first the trunk sections and then the spheres to the enormous "branches" of the Tree. Again an enormous crane was used to hoist the components into place while the two men went to work with their arc welding equipment. The trunk sections had to be welded together from inside the hollow tube-like form. Fearing that the men might suffocate or be overcome by the fumes generated by the welding process in such a confined space, Reimann operated a gas powered leaf-blower to force clean air into the base of the hollow structure. All noxious gasses, as well as the heat from the welding process, were then evacuated harmlessly and effectively from the top of the hollow trunk. The men later reported that they had experienced no discomfort during this arduous and potentially dangerous operation.

While overseeing the welding operation and tending to the continuous running of the life-sustaining leaf-blower, Reimann had time to reflect on his surroundings. He had never before been called upon to work in such a remote location with such desolate surroundings. He noticed the almost unbroken procession of car headlights that sped past the construction site toward Wendover on Friday evenings. During the day he watched dozens of jet contrails float motionlessly high in the clear blue sky, the only evidence of the passage of hundreds, perhaps even thousands, of unseen travelers as they hastened to their various destinations, oblivious to the drama of Momen's unfolding artistic endeavor. Always, he was aware of the bitingly cold wind that seemed to

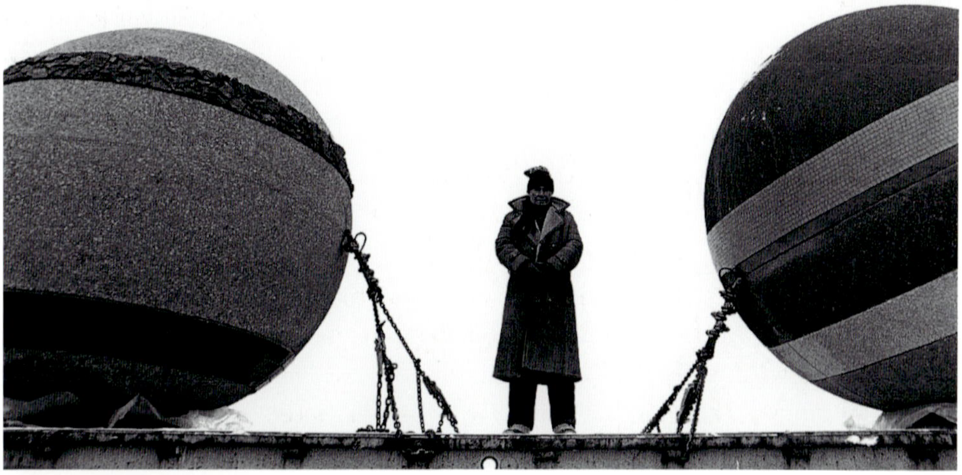

Momen stands on one of the flat-bed trucks that were used to transport the completed spheres across the desert to the construction site.

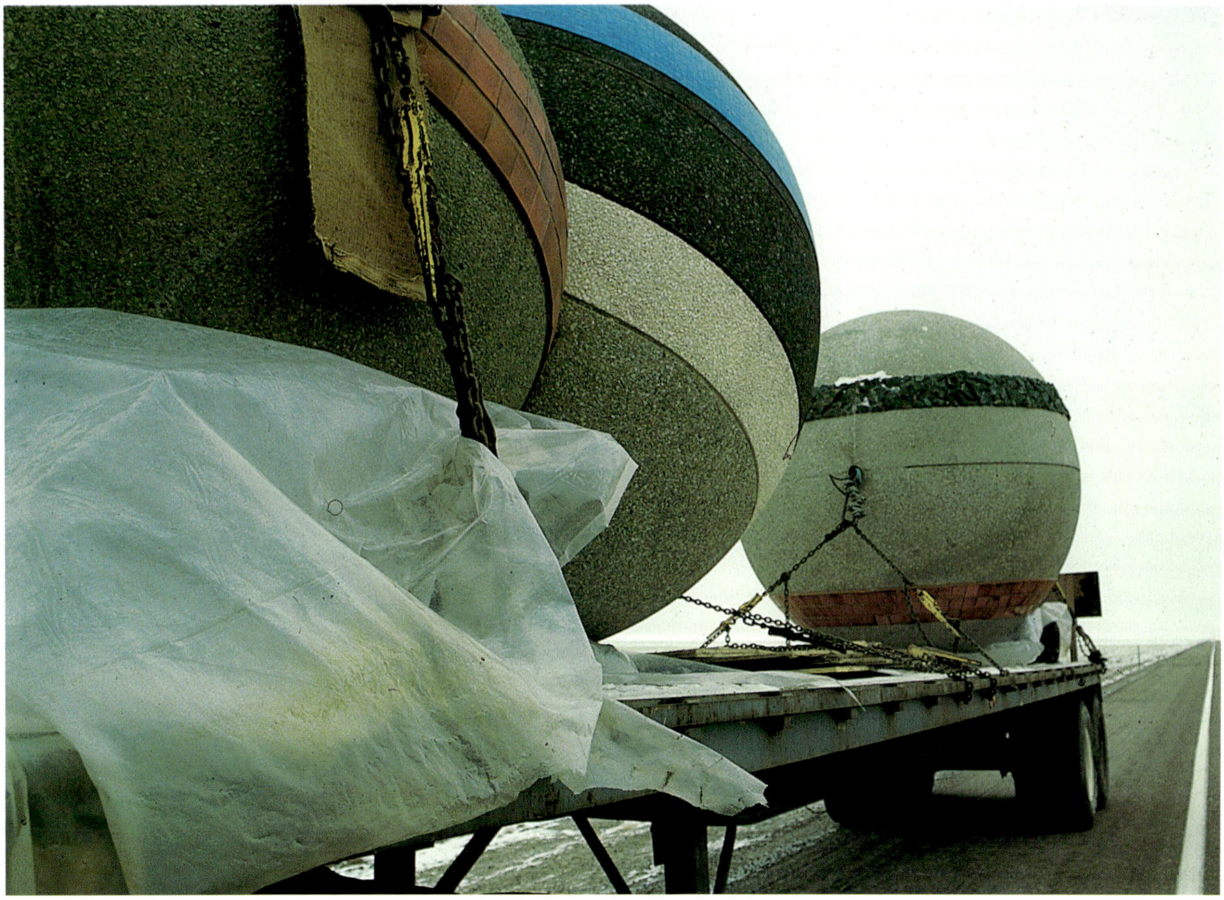

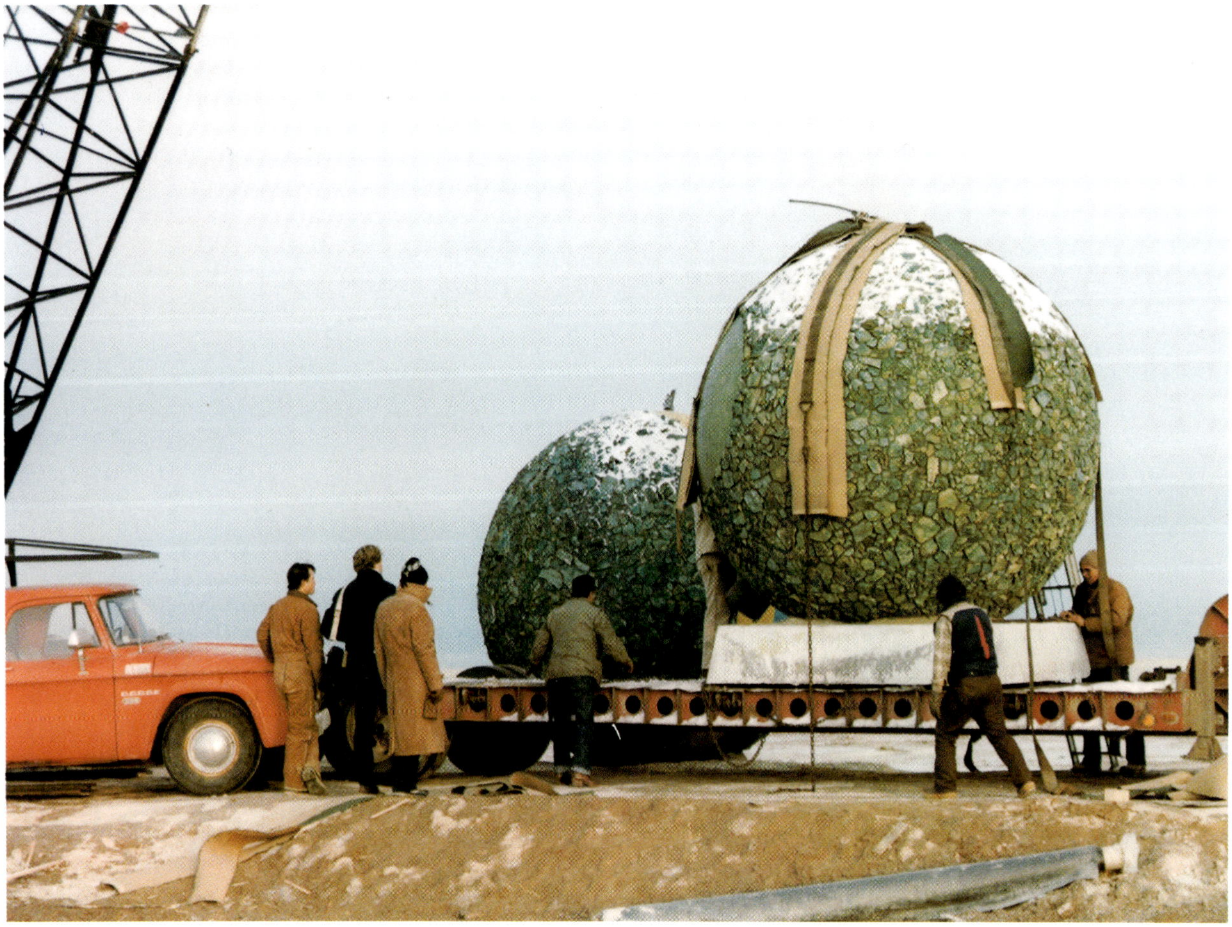

penetrate even his warmest clothing and left his face numb. After the trunk was welded together, it was poured full of concrete to maximize its structural integrity. The spheres were bolted and welded into position at the ends of enormous steel pipes that represented the "branches" of the Tree. All this work was accomplished in one period of two-and-a-half weeks. The end of the project was within Momen's grasp when Reimann discovered that the Tree would need cathodic protection to stop the steel reinforcing materials from being corroded by the saline environment of the Salt Flats. Reimann was able to find a company that specialized in this work. Momen was barely able to find the money for yet another unexpected expense. Then, in what seemed like a cruel twist of fate, just when Momen and his team thought that they had accounted for every outstanding contingency, they were informed that the structure would also have to be equipped with lightning protection. Miraculously, Momen scraped together the money for the installation of this equipment. Without adequate lightning protection the building authorities would not give their final approval to the structure. The equipment was installed and the construc-

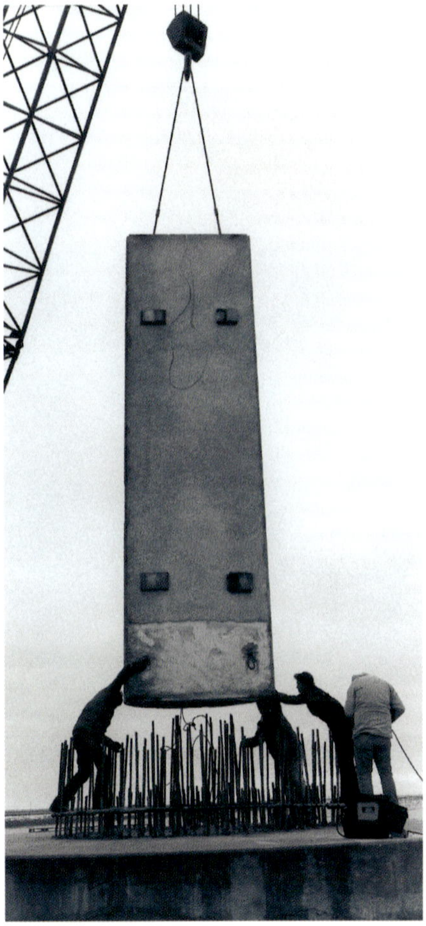

A large crane is used to lift the spheres off the flatbed trucks and to position the segments of the Tree's "trunk" before they are welded and fixed in place with a concrete girdle on top of the massive base.

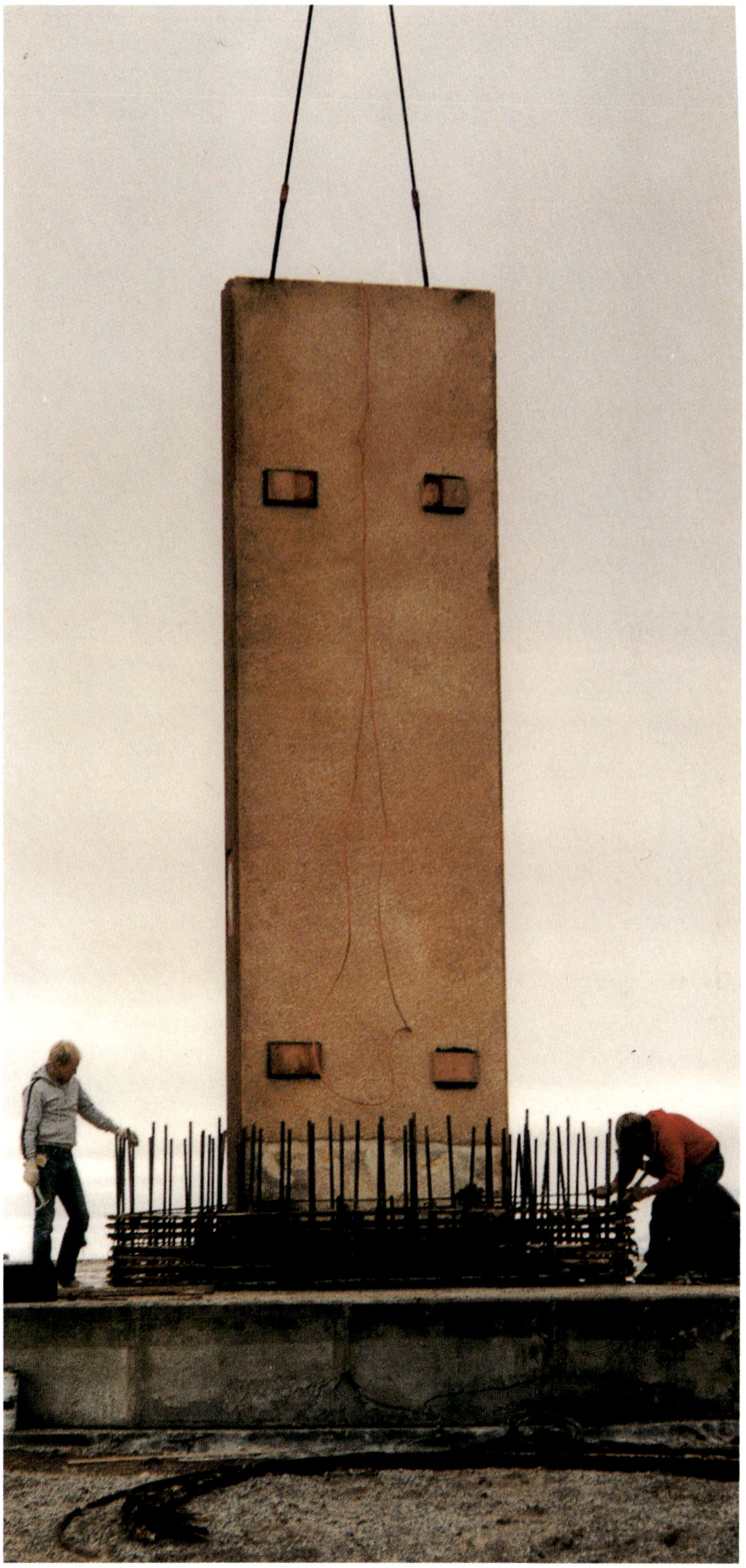

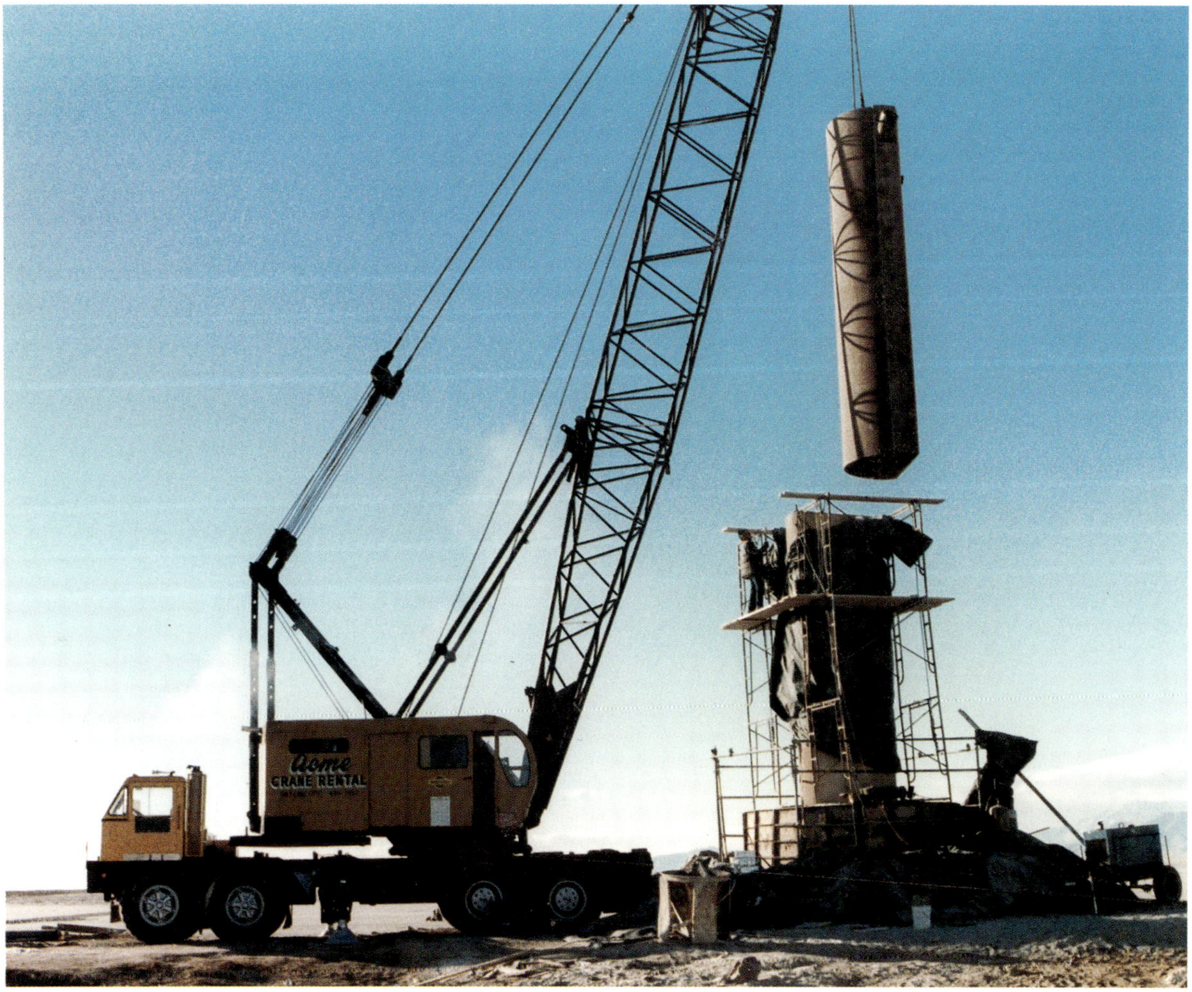

tion of the Tree of Utah was finally completed in September 1985. The finishing touches to the Tree had come just seventeen highly eventful months after work had commenced on the project.

The final bill of materials told its own story. In the end the project had consumed 100 tons of chrysocolla rock, 4 tons of epoxy, 160 tons of steel, 15 tons of colored cement, 18,000 imported ceramic tiles, 5 tons of welding rods, 7 tons of timber for mold formers, and 20 tons of plaster. The structure ended up weighing 875 tons and had consumed over 20,000 man-hours of labor. The project had cost Momen over $1 million in loaned funds and monies raised through the liquidation of his own assets. This figure was more than double the original estimates for the project. Don Reimann had built several impressive structures in Utah, however Momen's sculpture was the most challenging of all. His team had constructed it from start to finish with armatures and molds,

Above: *A crane lifts a segment of the Tree's "trunk" into position.*

Right: *Scaffolding was erected to allow workers to secure the spheres at the top of the "trunk."*

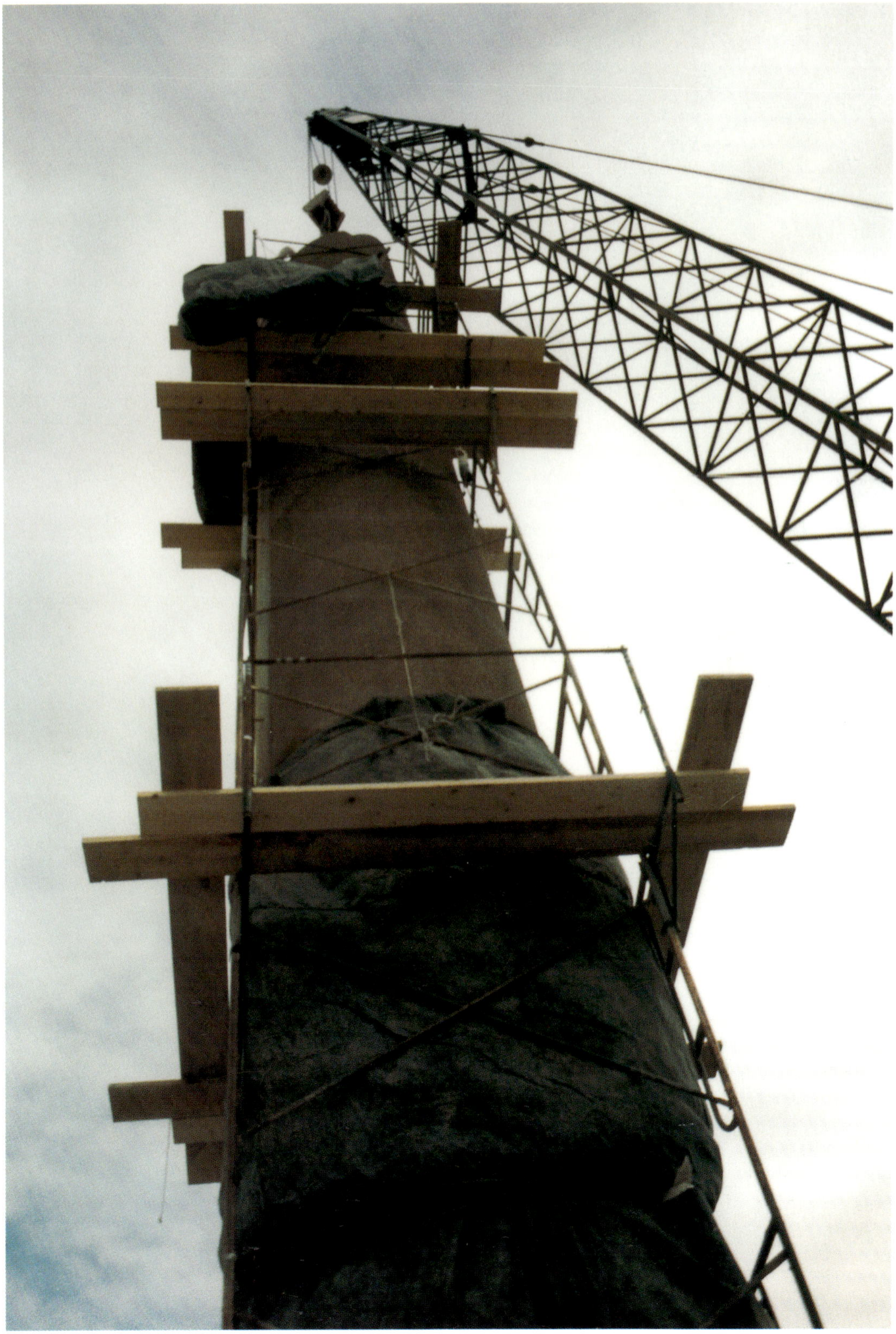

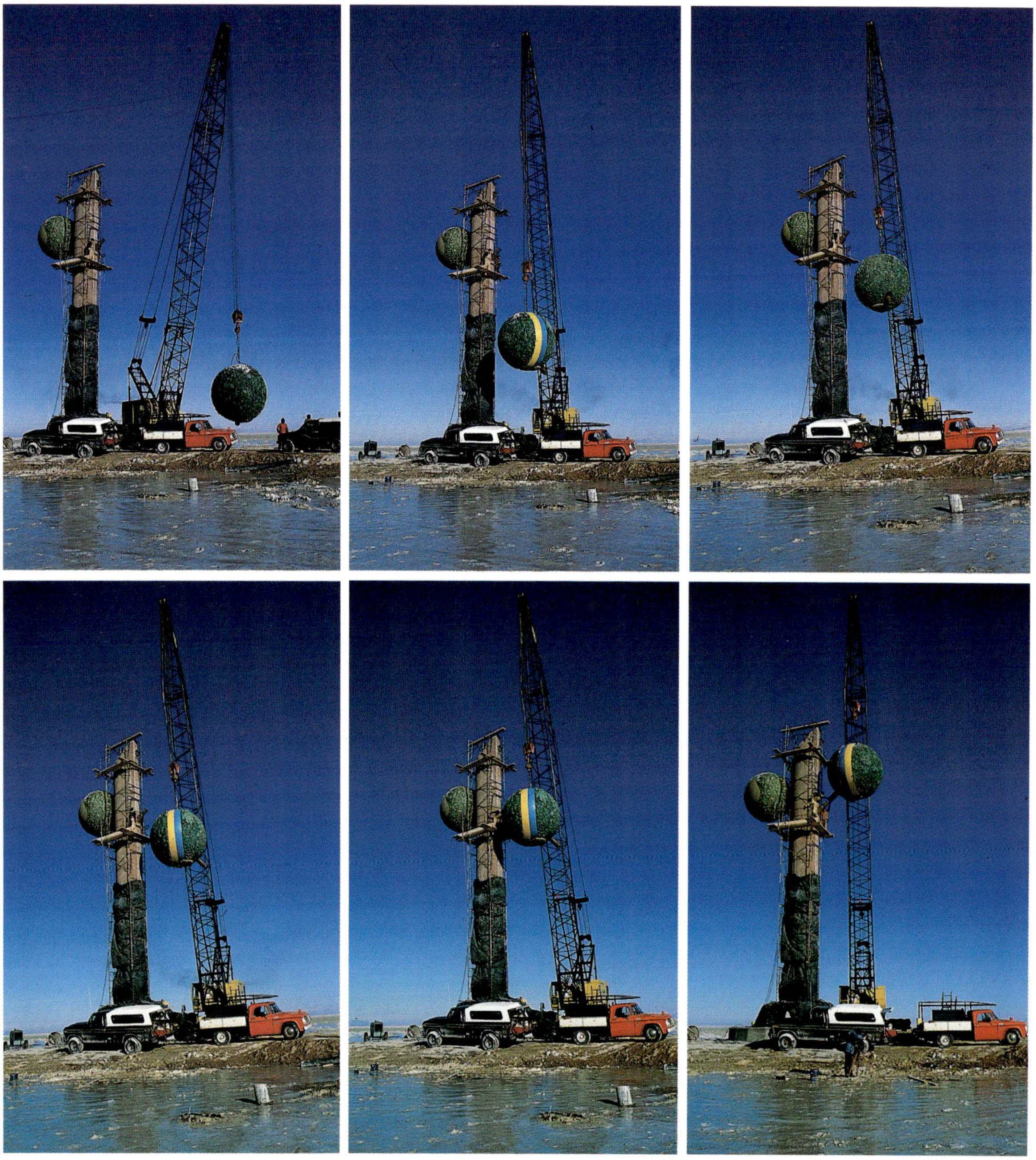

After the "trunk" is secured, the crane is used to carefully lift the heavy spheres into position.

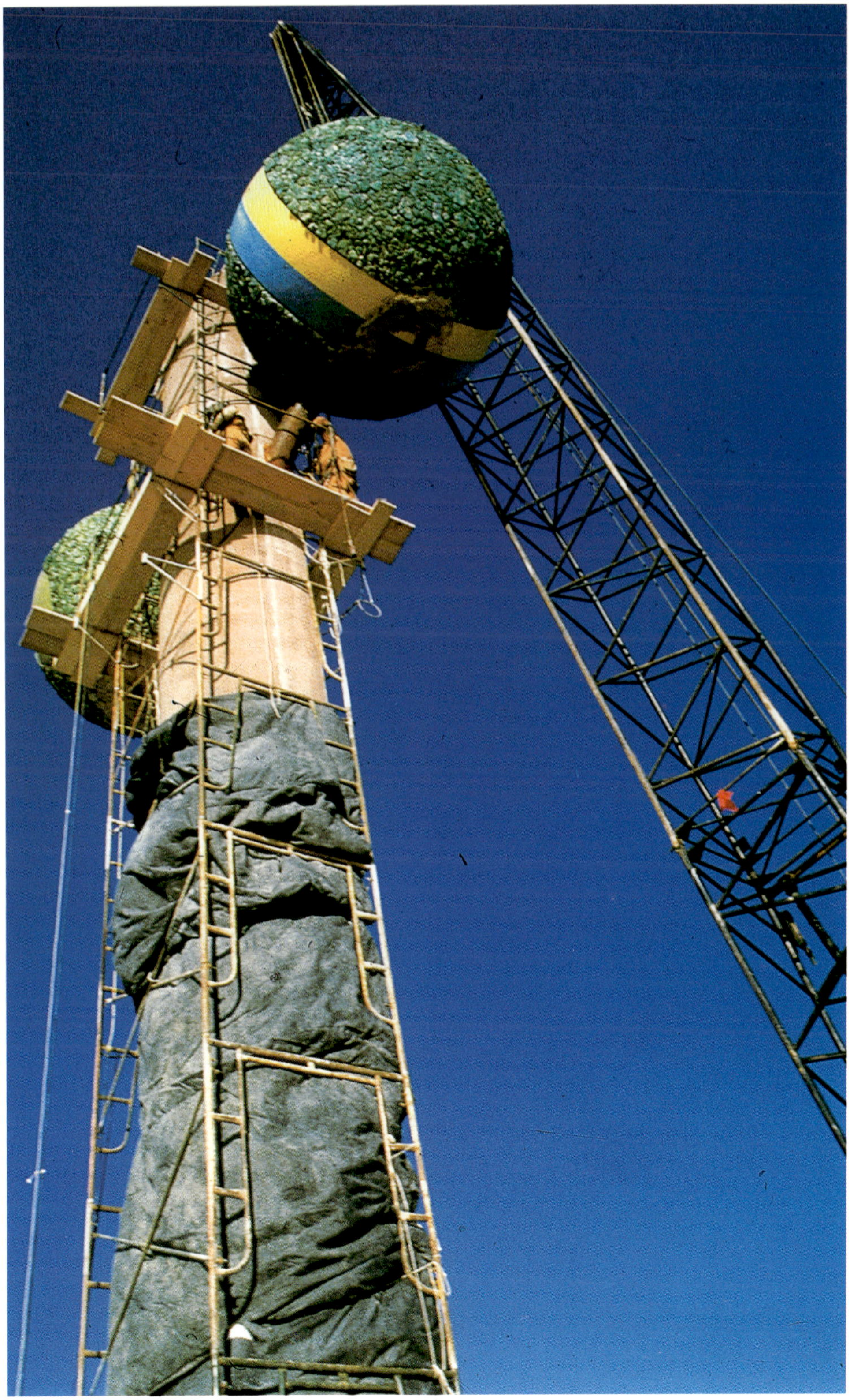

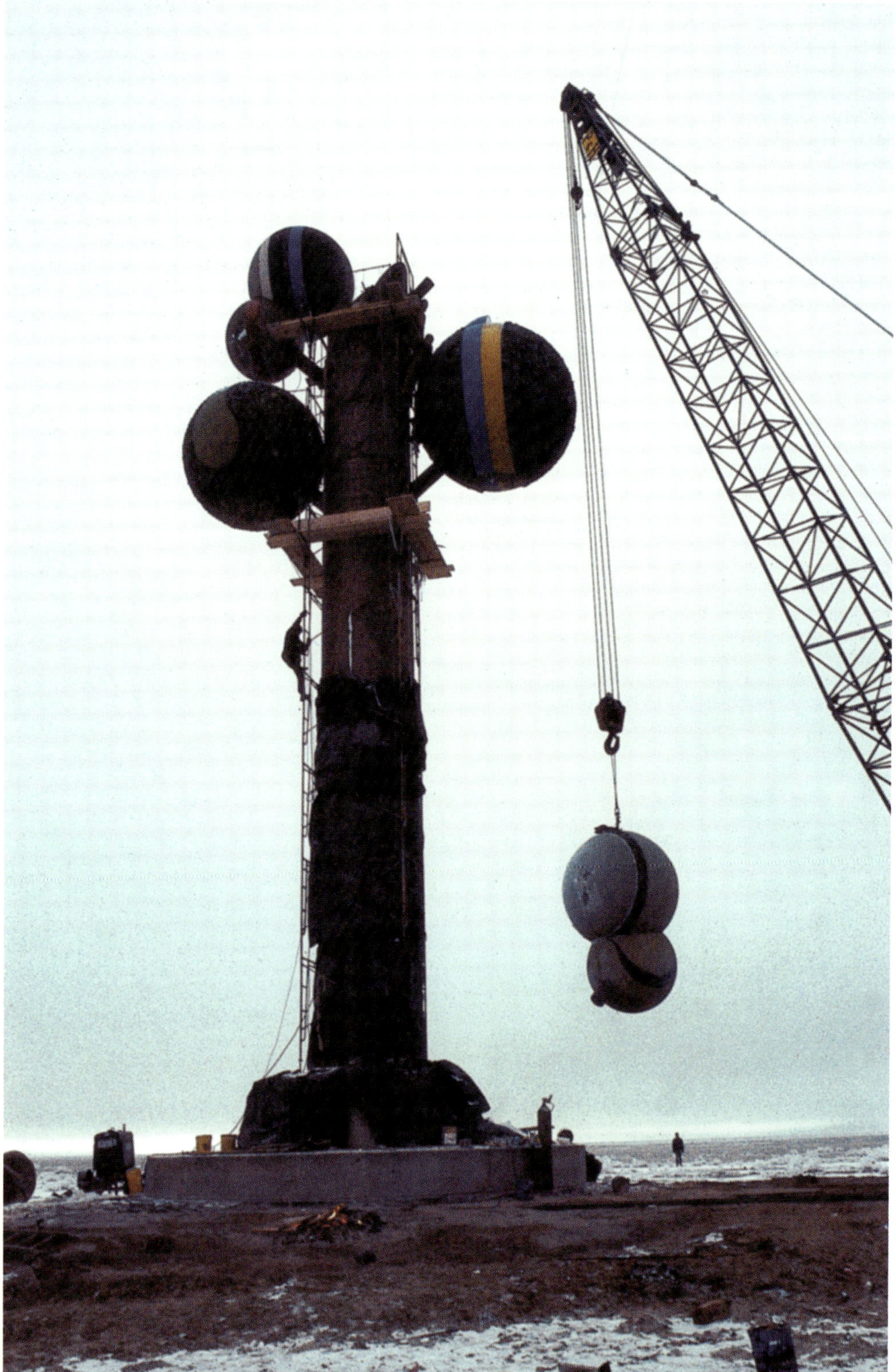

The Tree begins to take shape as the last spheres are lifted into position.

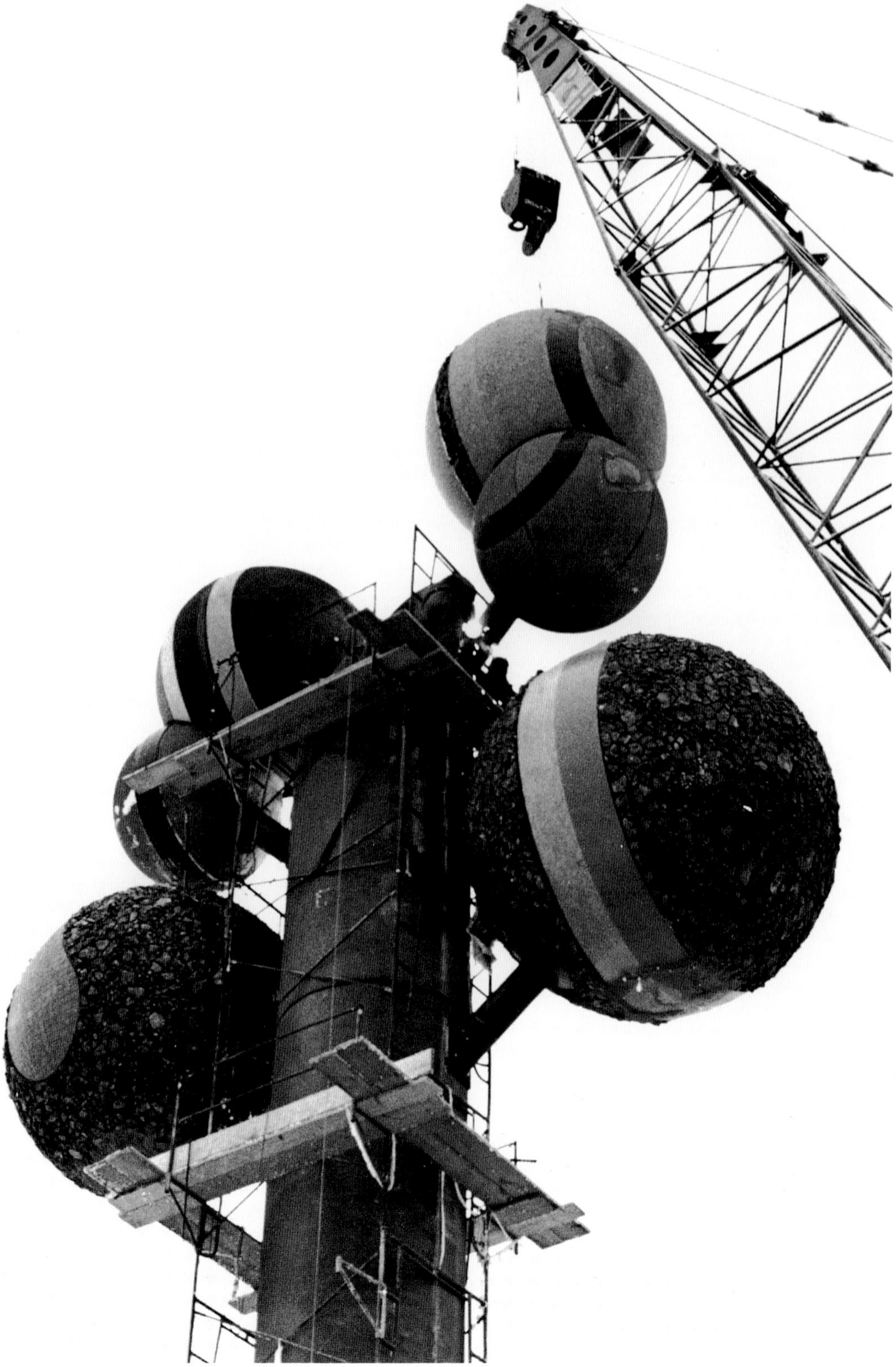

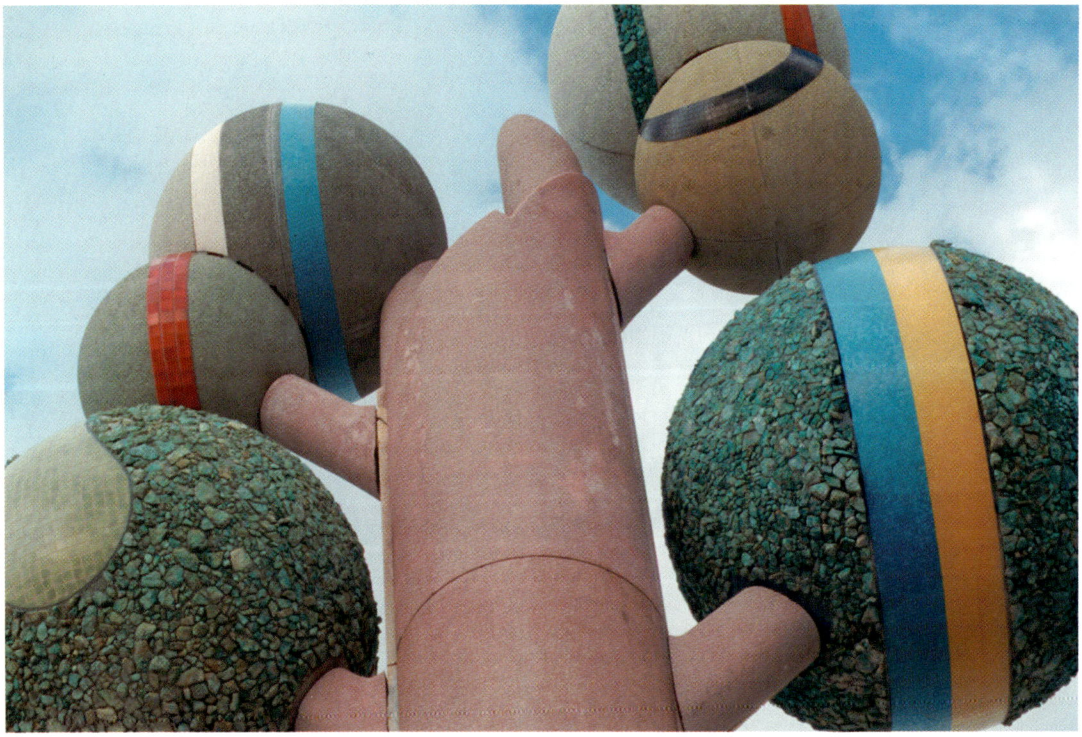

to the casting of the concrete spheres, and the final welding and erection of the structure in the desert. Momen could not believe how devoted and determined the Reimann family had been in completing this work.

Upon seeing the completed structure silhouetted against the stark Great Western Desert, Momen knew that his dream had been realized. However, in keeping with the character of his ever-restless spirit, he immediately turned his attention to organizing an opening event. He wanted to present his creation to the people of Utah. It was his sincere desire to see the Tree firmly placed within the cultural life of the state. A dedication ceremony was planned for Saturday, January 18, 1985. The Governor's office was contacted and invitations were sent to a wide range of civic leaders, artists and the arts organizations. The dedication ceremony would be presided over by Governor Norman Bangerter. Included in the invitation list was Carol Nixon, the recently appointed director of the Utah Arts Council, and Anna-Greta Leijon, the Swedish Minister of Labor who was visiting the country at the time. Momen would bear all the costs of the dedication, from renting the latrines for the public, to the helicopter used to fly the Governor to the event.

The dedication took place on a sunny Saturday morning. Over a thousand people gathered to the remote desert location to hear outgoing Utah Governor Norm Bangerter accept the "Tree of Utah" from its maker on behalf of the people of Utah. "I like it, it's

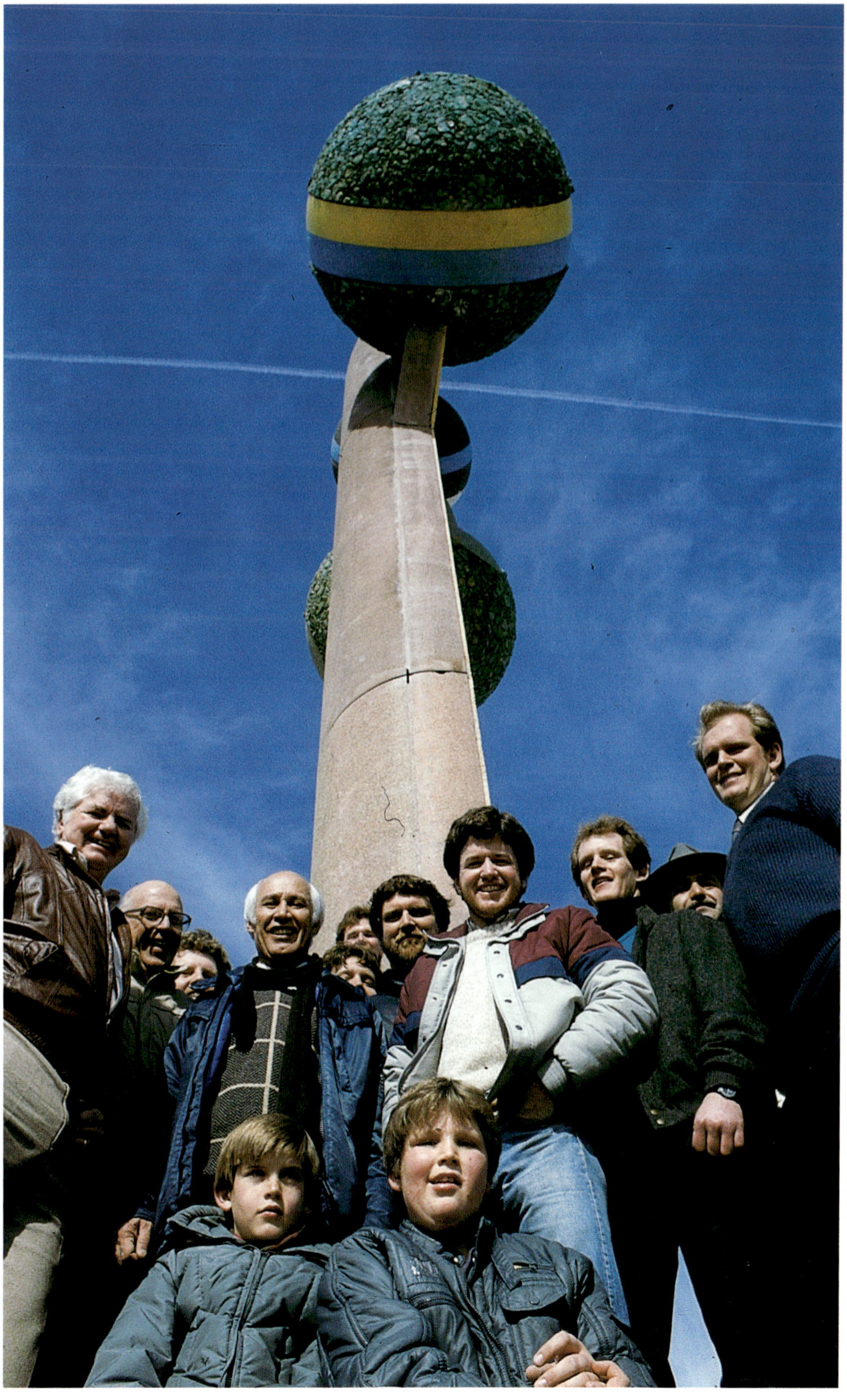

Momen poses with Don Reimann's family at the base of the Tree after safely completing the assembly of the Tree's components.

something different—distinctly different" he noted in his remarks. A wide range of people from many different walks in life attended the event. The Swedish Minister of Labor had interrupted her itinerary to participate in the occasion. Momen had heard that she was in the United States on a business visit. He found out where he could contact her and sent her an invitation, which she accepted on the spur of the moment. Also in the audience were many of the Utah art establishment, including maestro Joseph Silverstein's wife, and others with no artistic pretensions who simply found the Tree intriguing and strangely satisfying. The Tree had the power to bring a heterogeneous group of people together who shared nothing more than a common interest in the manifestation of a particular aesthetic sensibility. There was nothing to be gained materially from their interest, yet it filled their imaginations with a particular perception that some described as "quite delightful" and another as "very deep." At this event the State of Utah became the unwitting recipient of one of its most intriguing manmade structures, donated by a foreign visitor who had spontaneously committed to the crea-

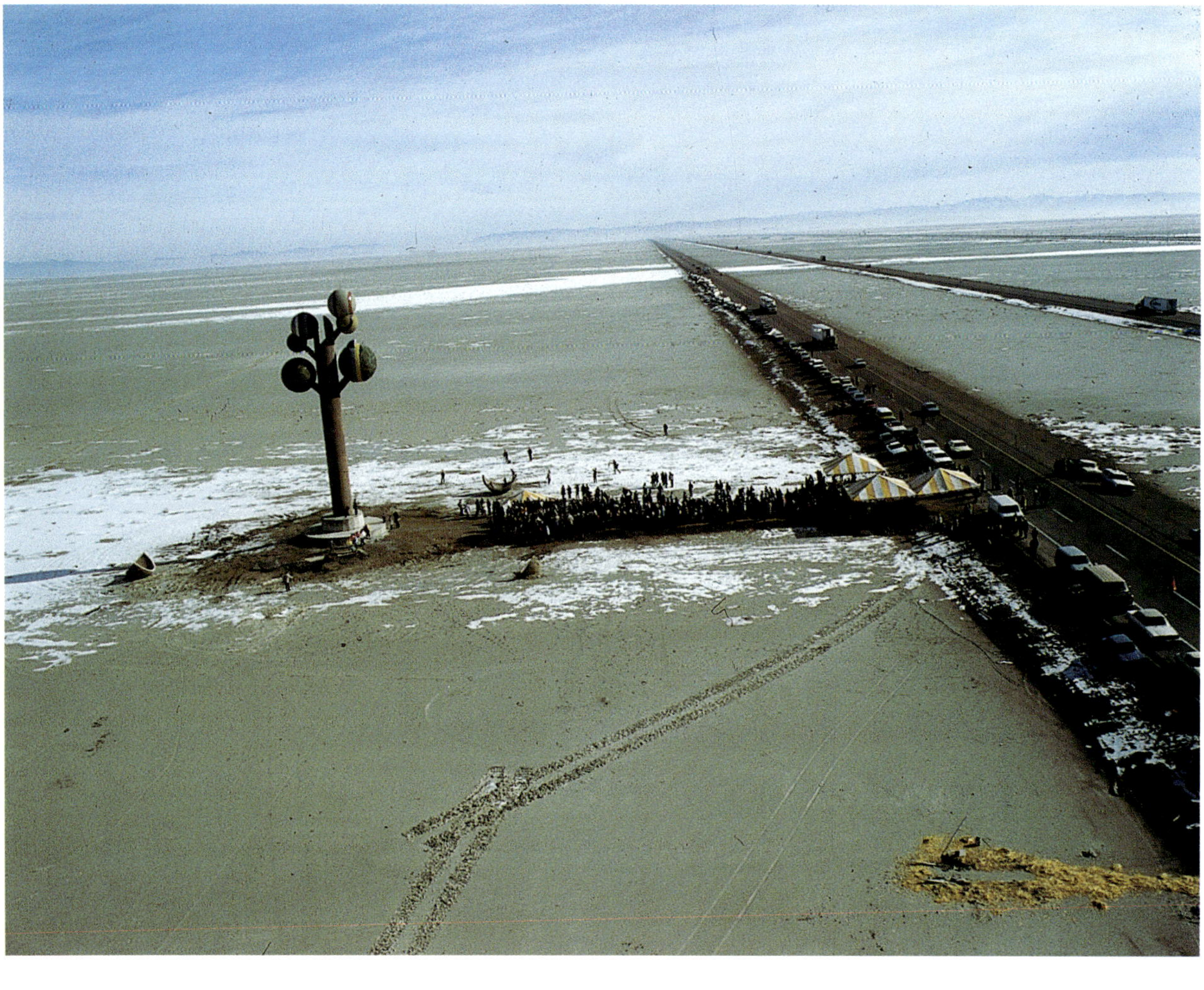

Cars and busses line up on the shoulder of Interstate 80 and Governor Bangerter's party arrives by helicopter to attend the Tree's dedication ceremony.

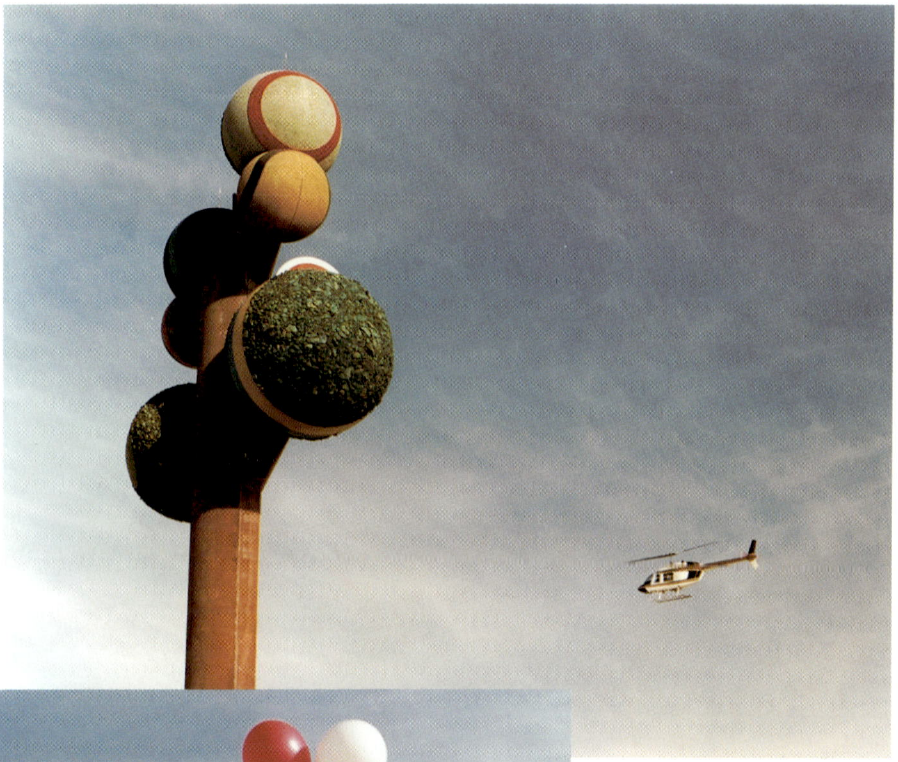

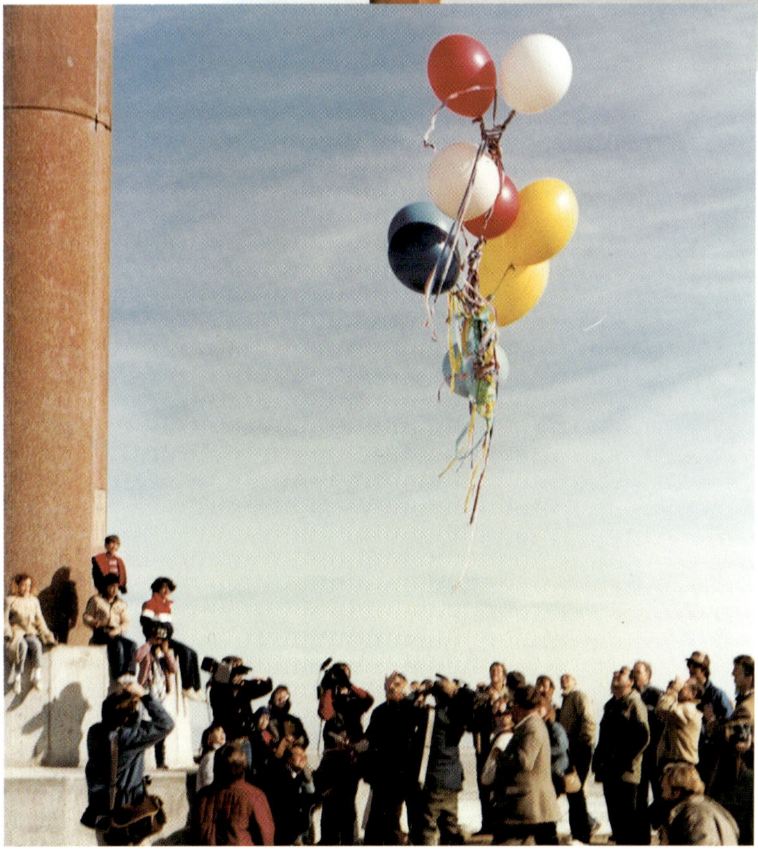

Overleaf: *Several hundred people ventured out to attend the dedication gala in the desert.*

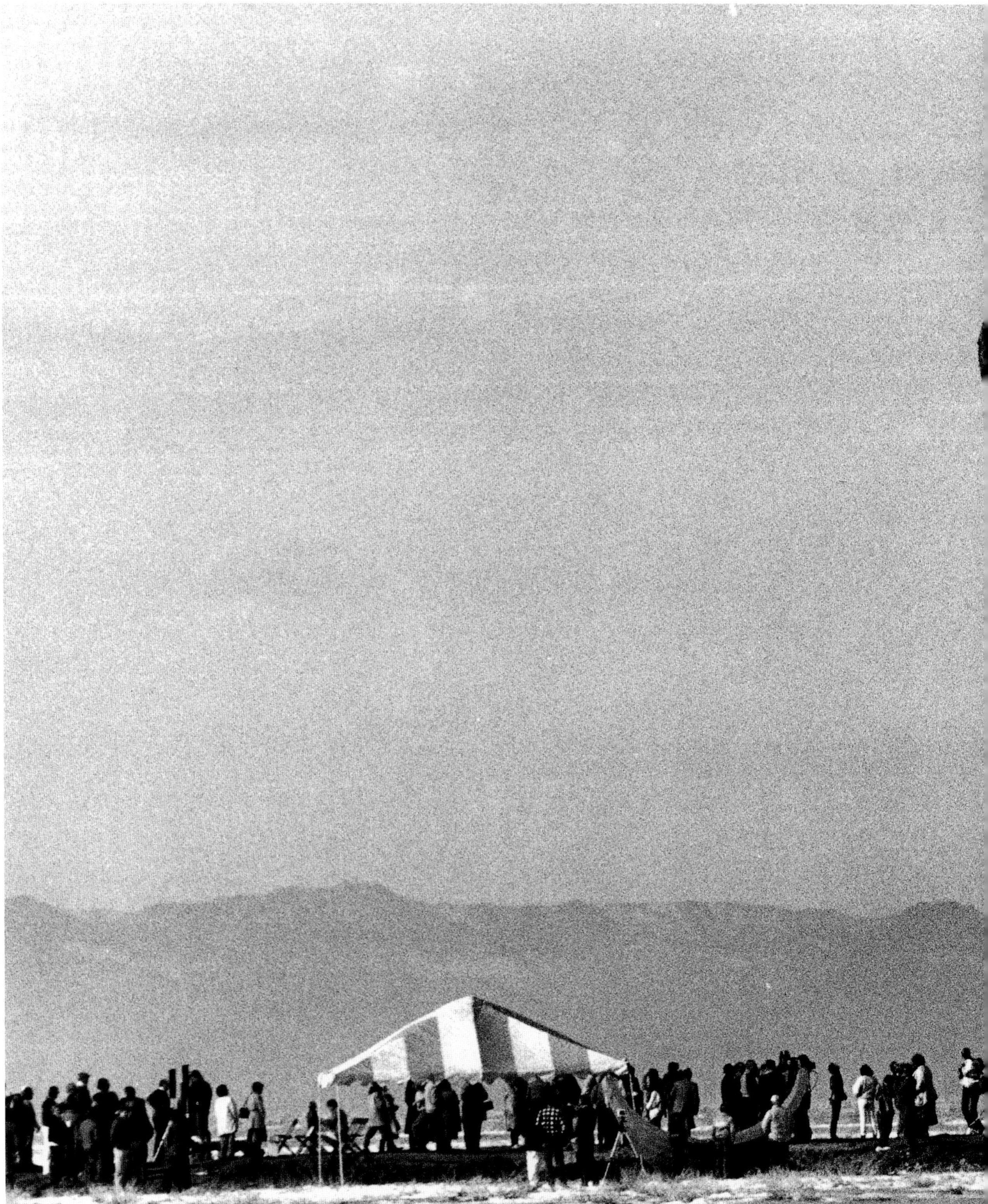

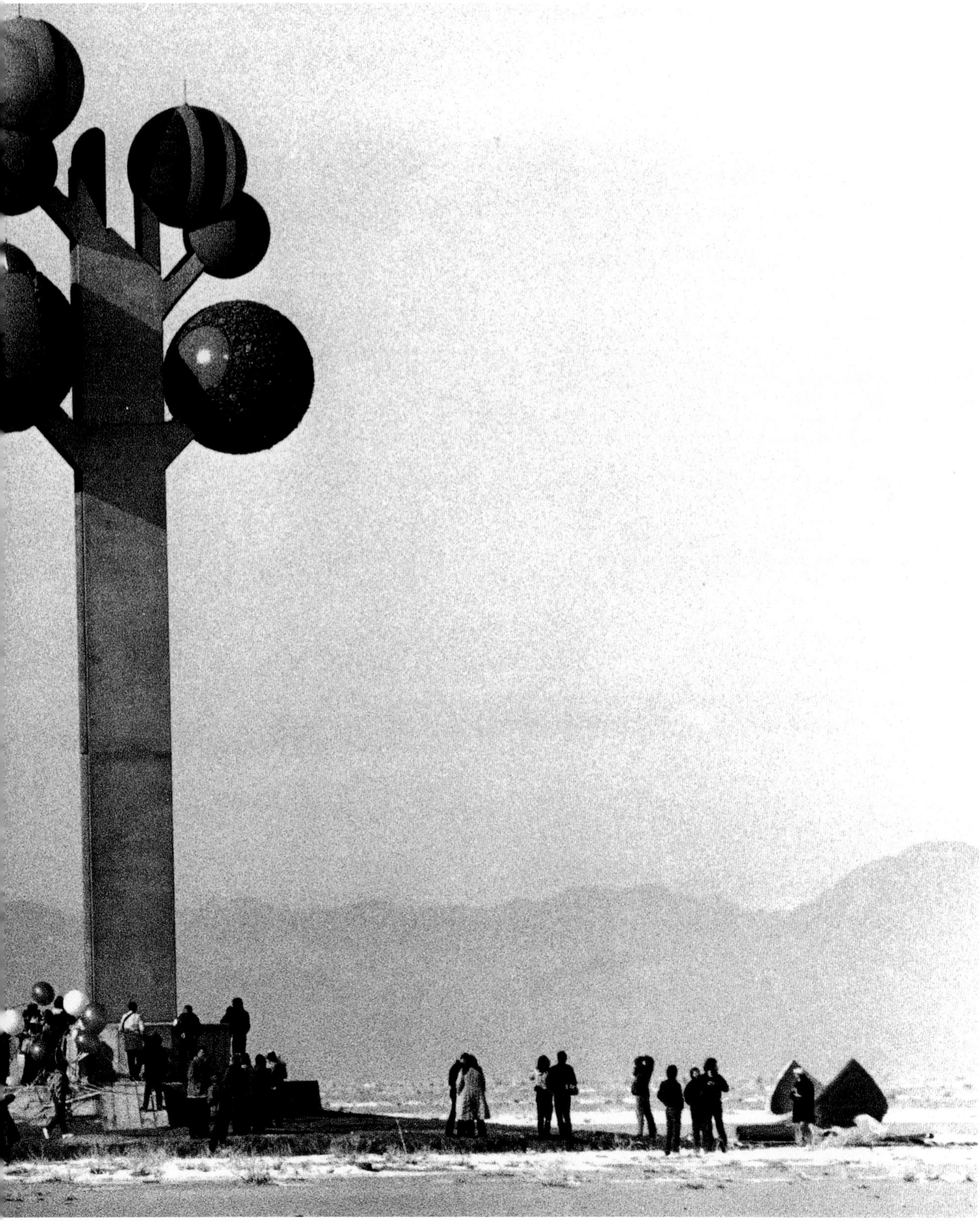

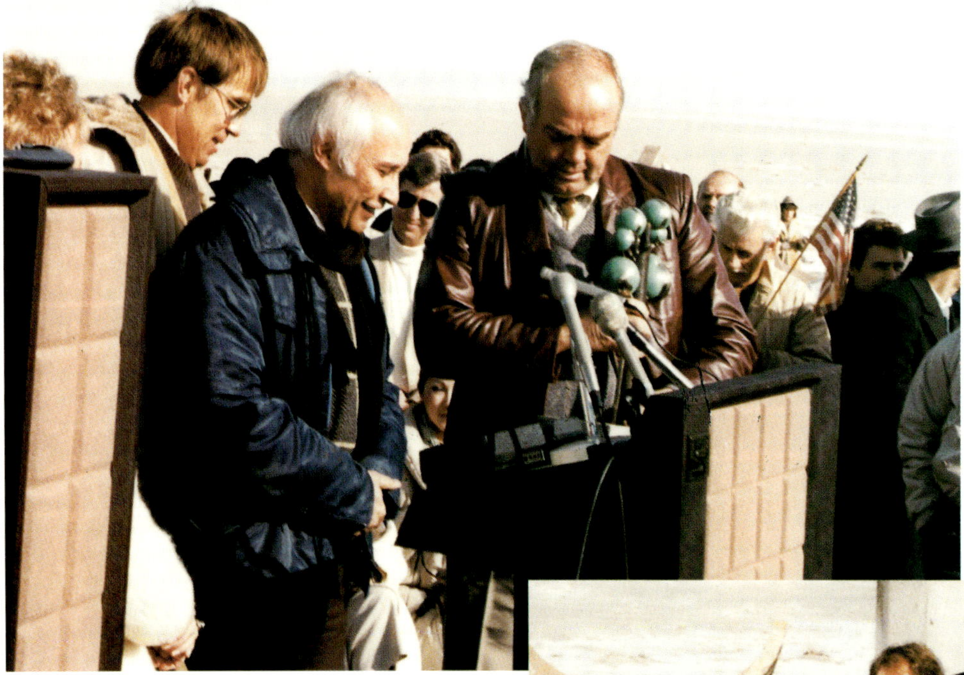

Left: *Momen joins Governor Norman Bangerter at the podium during the dedication ceremony.*

Below: *Prominent Utah artists who supported the project from the beginning. Dennis Smith, Neil Hadlock, Gary Smith.*

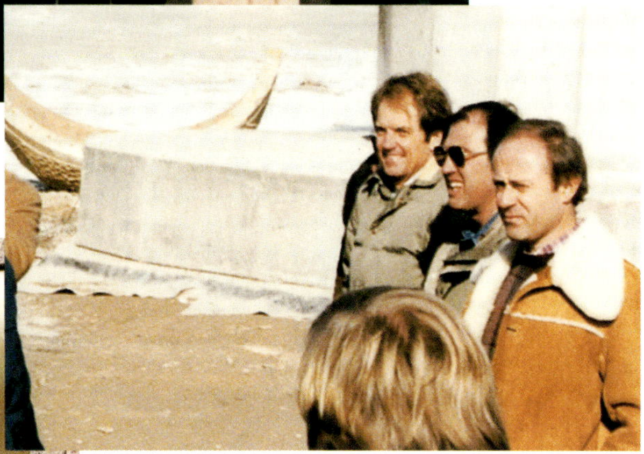

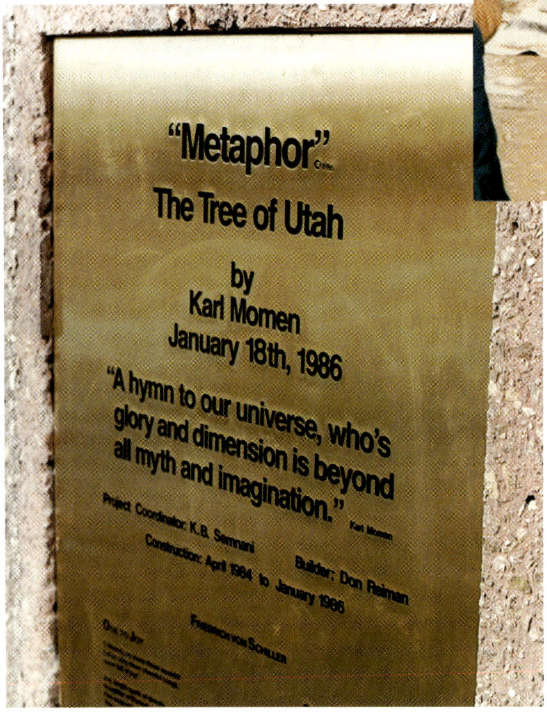

Left: *The bronze plaque installed on the trunk of the Tree reads; "A hymn to our universe, who's (sic) glory and dimension is beyond all myth and imagination."*

This inscription is followed by Friedrich von Schiller's, "Ode to Joy."

The plaquette was later stolen. Hopefully for its sentimental value as a token, not for the price of the bronze.

tion of a unique and surprisingly appropriate tribute to the stark and featureless Great Western Desert. Governor Bangerter, assisted by Carol Nixon, had the good grace to accept Momen's magnanimous gesture notwithstanding the cultural conservatism of this state and the reticence of local authorities to come to terms with such an extraordinary manifestation of an individual artist's vision and resourcefulness. In this respect Momen's project epitomized a victory of the creative spirit over the stultifying strictures of an impassive economic system that threatened to bankrupt the project; an alienated mass media that tried to denigrate and sensationalize the project, and the negativism of an essentially conservative and uninformed public. Those who attended the dedication ceremony enjoyed a celebratory atmosphere that drew many favorable comments. Carol Nixon and the Governor thoroughly enjoyed the occasion and good feelings were shared by all. It truly was a celebration of the arts. Ironically the state had no mechanism at this time to legally receive the Tree into its care. This was only accomplished on September 25, 1996, when the new Utah Governor of the state, Mike Leavitt formally and finally accepted Momen's donation of the sculpture and the land after the necessary legal work had been accomplished by the state. They had never had to deal

Momen chats while environmentalists protest silently in the background.

Seated from left: *Dennis Smith, Chairman of Visual Art Committee, Utah Arts Council, Momen, Mrs Bangerter, Governor Bangerter, Mrs Carol Nixon Director of Utah Arts Council, Miss Carol Eng.*

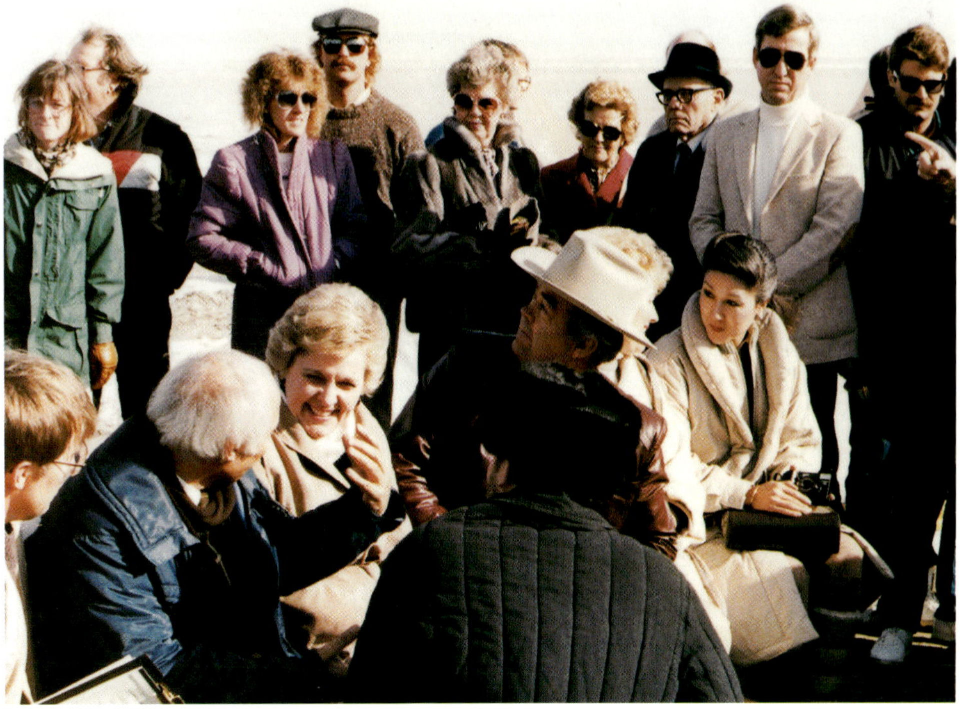

Overleaf: *Governor Norman Bangerter welcomes Anna Greta Leijon, the Swedish Minister of Labor, before the dedication.*

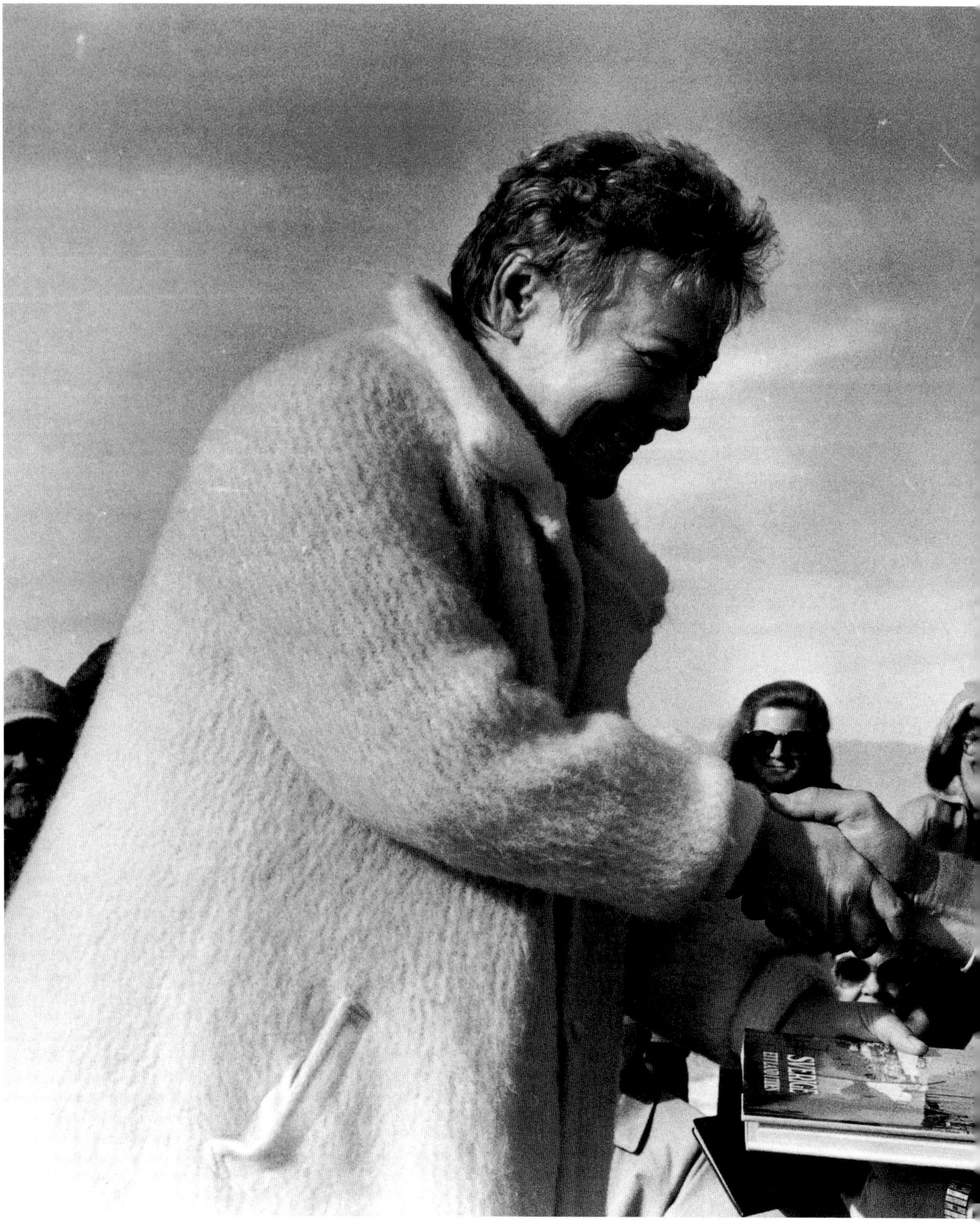
SVERIGE

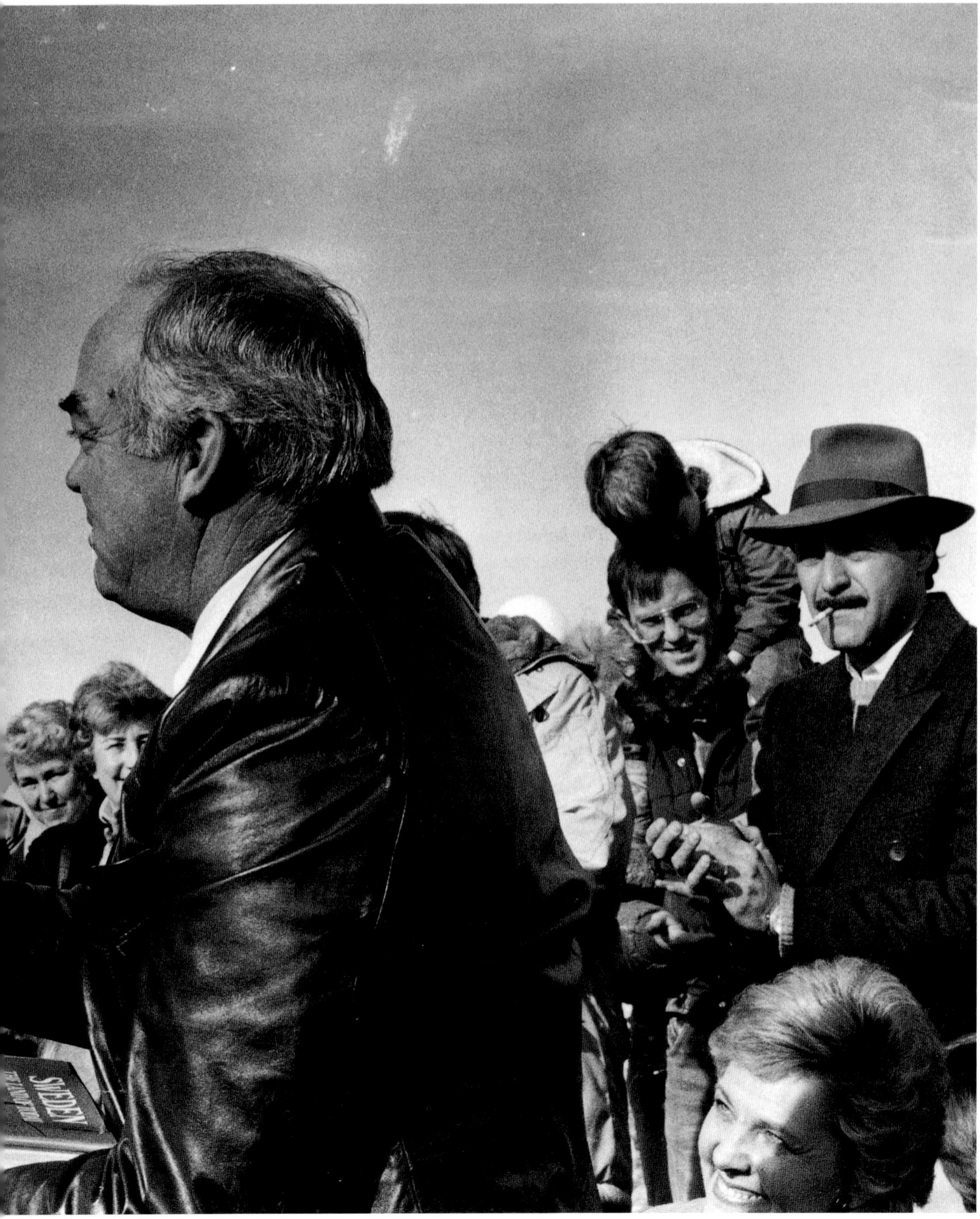
SWEDEN

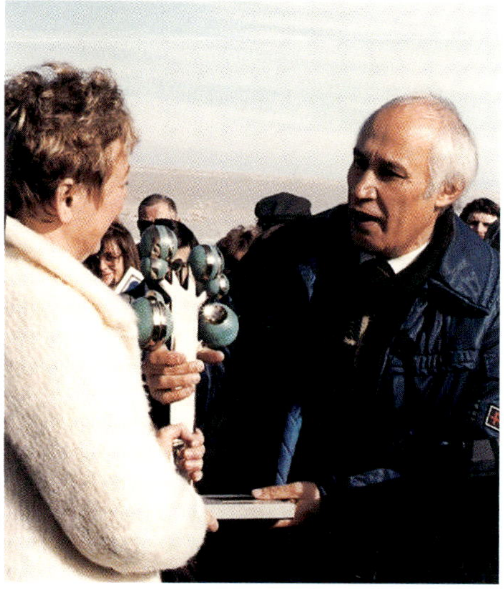

We leave New York and travel to Washington for discussions with the government and a reception at the home of the Swedish Labor Market Council Mr.Henry Persson. There, I receive an odd looking letter. It is from Utah, Salt Lake City, and the sender's name is Momen. My first thought associates him with the Mormons, who have their headquarters there. Perhaps it is just a piece of advertising or propaganda. Since the letter is brought to me by an embassy official I open it anyway and I read it. In a way it is an advertisement but in a different way than I thought. The letter is long and the contents more or less as follows:

"Your Excellency,
My name is Karl Momen, architect and artist, Swedish citizen, however born in former Persia. I know that this Saturday you will be flying to California. If you leave early in the morning it would be possible for you to make a stopover in Salt Lake City to attend the inauguration of my Tree sculpture in the Great Salt Desert. This would be a great honor to me. The Governor and I will meet you with a helicopter."

It sounds like a real adventure. The travel itinerary is changed. We choose the morning flight. At the airport in Salt Lake City Karl Momen meets with us, he appears to be a distinguished gentleman a bit over 50 years of age. The helicopter is standing by but it is a small model and the Governor is flying ahead in his own.

The large white and gray salt desert lies surrounded by high mountain chains. A straight highway has been constructed across it. I am told it takes a couple of hours to drive through the desert. Here, a few years earlier Karl Momen came along in his car. He had a tomato for travel food and thought it would be nice with a grain of salt. He had only to stop the car and get a few crystals from the ground. Momen looked around over the empty landscape. "This place needs a sculpture," he thought and pondered on who would be able to make a piece of art for the desert stretching for miles and miles none other than himself, obviously!

Karl Momen's giant project started to take shape. There was to be a tree. A tree with a form he had used in other contexts. Probably, only an architect and a world citizen understands what the desert demands. It is not a skinny little tree. Nor is it tall and lofty like a poplar. It is a powerful broad-shouldered tree where the leafage is shaped into large round spheres. The tree is almost 27 meters high, stabilized 30 meters down and mainly constructed in cement. The material and the colors must withstand rain, snow and storm winds full of salt. To plant such a tree in the salt desert is expensive business requiring sponsors. Coca-Cola promises support. But not until the tree is almost finished is the demand forwarded to place a billboard on the upper sphere. But that was not the vision in Karl Momen's mind the day he had his tomato as a snack. Karl Momen rejects Coca-Cola and makes good his expenses by selling his cottage in Lofsdalen in the Swedish mountains, his stamp collection, and goes into debt for the rest of the money. He is looking ahead counting on receipts, for instance, from the TV-companies that are monitoring the construction of the tree.

About 700 people have arrived to be present at the inauguration. The tree "grows" 85 miles west of Salt Lake City. Balloons play in the wind together with Swedish and American flags. Present are also several TV-teams and a couple of demonstrators from the Green Movement who do not want any human intrusion in the salt desert. The Governor is a real governor complete with cowboy hat, leather stripes for a tie and spurs on his boots. The Governor, the chairman of the Board of Culture, and myself are giving speeches. TV is filming and the audience shivers a bit in the wind but gives applause and cheers.

Karl Momen has had a remarkable life. Already as a small boy he demonstrated artistic talent and at 12 years old he portrays Stalin. Later he gets an opportunity to also paint the Shah of Iran. "Both portraits have been used as doormats," he states humorously and with this catches some of the drama of our present history.

From Anna Greta Leijon's autobiography:
"Alla rosor ska inte tuktas!" (All roses need not to be punished) 1991. pp 211-213.

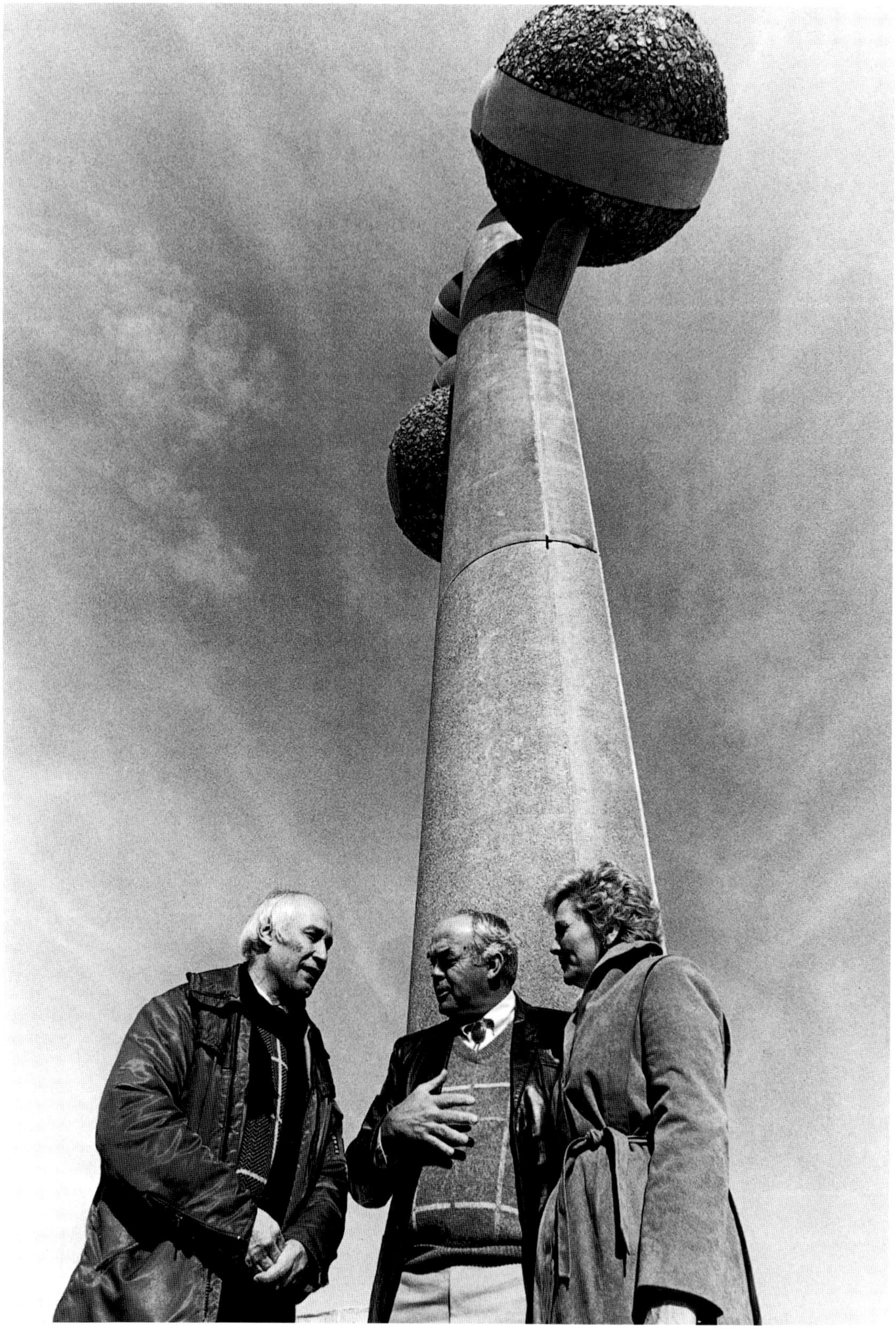

Left: *Momen discuss his creation with Governor and Mrs. Bangerter.*

with such a case before. However, even after the legality of the Tree had been resolved, the Utah Department of Transport (UDOT)—the state authority that administers this section of highway—found it extremely difficult to work out a satisfactory solution for the maintenance of the site and to make it amenable to travelers who wished to visit it. By mid-1999 four years after the official acceptance by the state of its responsibility there was still no planned maintenance of the site of any kind. Nor was there any provision for motorists to stop at the site to view the sculpture; in fact it was a traffic offence punishable by state law to even stop one's vehicle along this section of the I-80 highway. In his engaging and innovative fashion Momen had, over the years, come up with plans that would provide income for the maintenance of the Tree and its site. However, these plans were contingent upon the construction of a turn-out that would allow motorists to stop at the site and purchase postcards, posters, and other souvenirs. Estimates for this work ran into the millions of dollars and apparently the state was not prepared to foot the bill. Momen even had plans for an international sculpture park at the site that would attract world famous sculptors' and their works. The nature of future developments are still unresolved, however the Tree of Utah has come to stay. Who knows what future generations will think of its maker and those who were associated with its planning and construction? In the meanwhile it has become a true metaphor for our engagement with this beautiful and elemental portion of the world that we live on.

Overleaf: *The Tree of Utah seen above its mirrored image after a rare rain storm in the desert.*

Photo: François Camoin

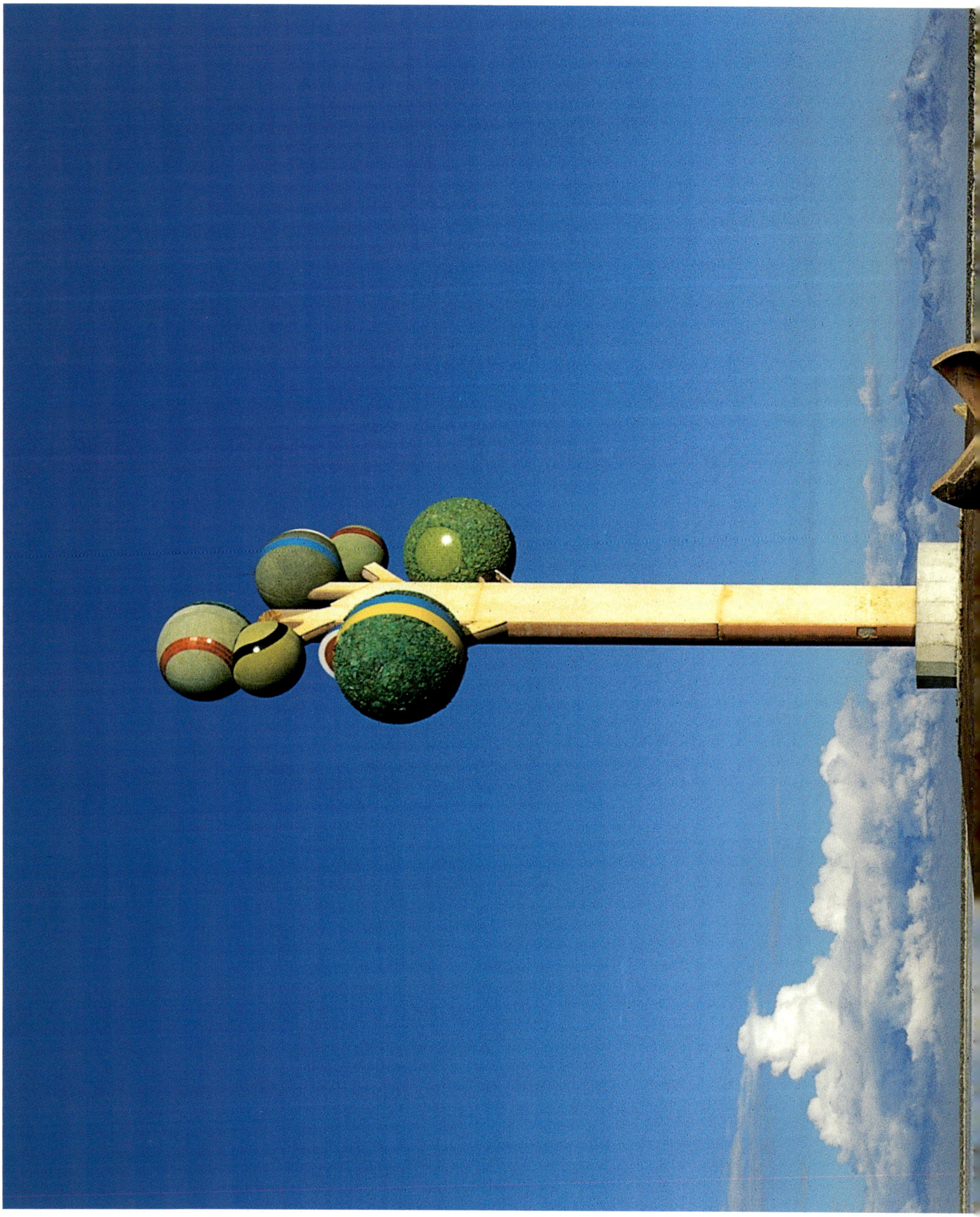

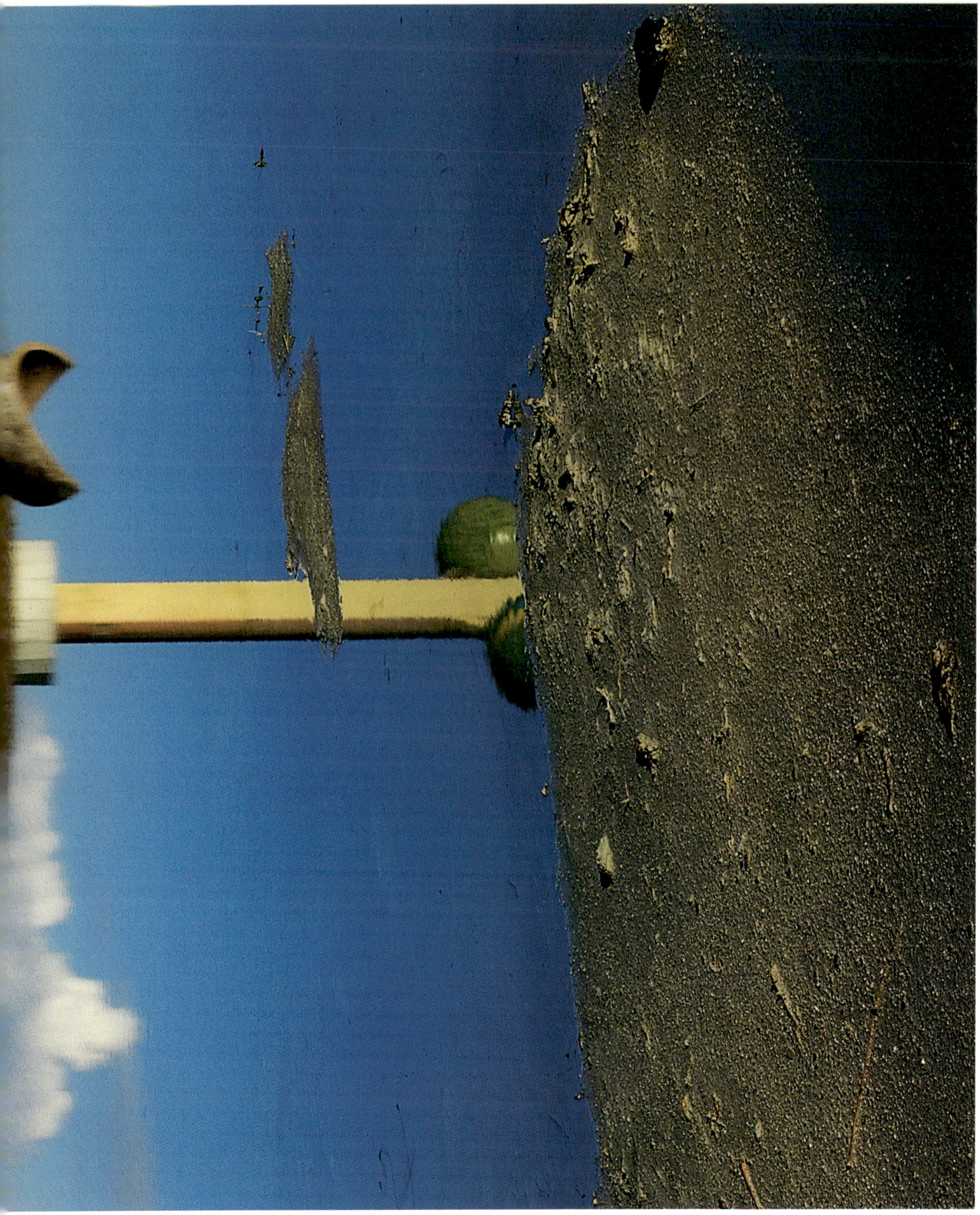

Chapter seven

CONTRARY VOICES AND PRAISE SINGERS

Even before ground had been broken for the foundation of the Tree, media interest had descended on the project, straining to identify any aspect that could lead to something sensational that would gain ascendancy over the plethora of other "stories" that permeate the news media at all times. Newspaper headlines such as: *Tree artist wants to put more flavor in the 'salt'* and *Utah Mulls over Karl Momen's Monumental Meatballs*, proliferated. Not to be outdone, the Wall Street Journal carried a headline that read: *Sure, the Redwoods Grow Taller, But They Don't Have Coconuts*. Other writers referred to the Tree as "a coagulated mushroom cloud" or as "giant scoops of ice-cream." These statements by the media were indicative of the derisive attitude adopted by many critics as they applied their own sensibilities to the task of interpreting the Tree to their largely uninformed readers. Similes of "meatballs," "ice-cream scoops," and "coconuts" drawn from the kitchen gives a fair indication of the area of the human anatomy that these particular critics applied to their analysis. Many of these often self-appointed critics took it upon themselves to voice their condemnation of the Tree simply because it was something that had suddenly sprung up within their midst, was contrary to anything that they had experienced before, and therefore difficult to accept.

These critics often lacked the conceptual apparatus to adequately contextualise the sculpture, or to apply appropriate constructs to its interpretation. It is also a fact that there had been no "buy-in" by the public. The public had never been consulted or invited to contribute to the realization of Momen's idea. Derision is often the response of those who feel left out or disadvantaged for not being able to make sense of something that others appear to understand and hold in high esteem. It is true that no significant measure of talent or aptitude is required to find fault or to criticize another's endeavors. Significantly, several well-known and respected local artists, namely Frank Riggs, Gary

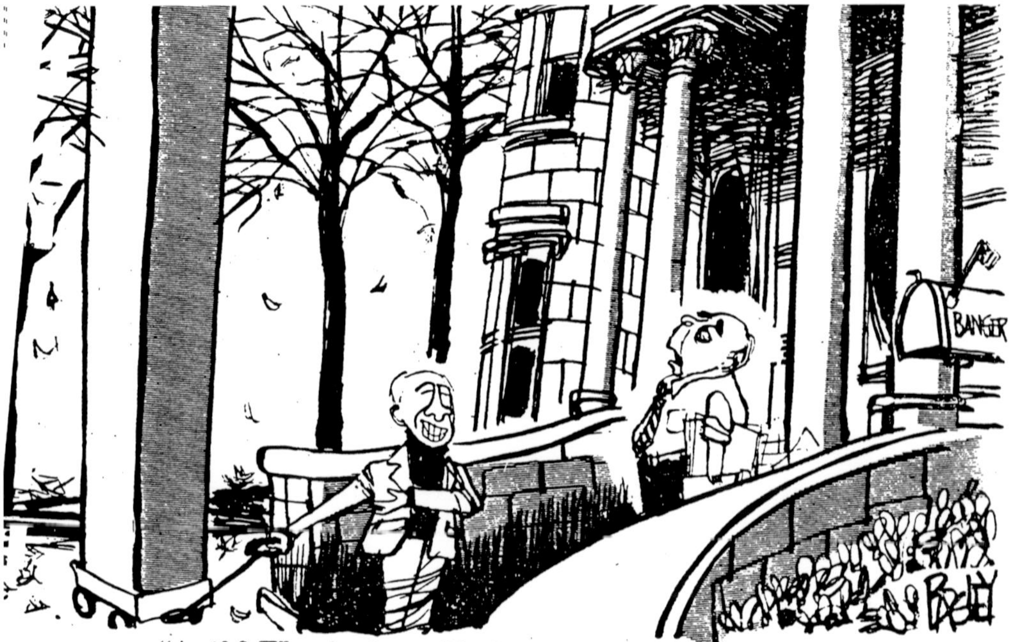

"A gift? Why thank you Mr. Momen. It's very, ummm...*big*!
You really shouldn't have. N<u>o</u>, really, I mean it."

This cartoon whimsically captured the reticence of the local community to Momen's gift.

Courtesy of
The Salt Lake Tribune

Smith, Dennis Smith, and Neil Hadlock—all gave their support throughout the project.

Although the Tree stood in a swirl of local controversy, worldwide interest was also aroused, and more than 600 individual publications would eventually carry news of the Tree. The Swedish press gave the Tree intense media coverage because of Momen's Swedish citizenship. The Japanese media also showed surprising interest. Numerous articles appeared in art and architecture magazines. Significantly, overseas interest was more informed and more positive than local reports. Many local media reports sought to sensationalize their accounts of the Tree, often presenting the Tree as a bizarre phenomenon. Ironically the Tree may have attracted more critical awareness overseas than in Utah itself. It was perhaps for this reason that Elaine Jarvik, a local critic, noted that the Tree of Utah was arguably Utah's most visible and internationally well known artwork. The growing awareness of the Tree by the public media prompted some advertisers to think of the Tree as a ready made advertising opportunity; it could qualify as one of the world's most striking billboards. Momen received proposals from some Nevada casinos to hang signs from the boughs of the Tree. He also received offers from film companies to film commercials at the site and to build a snack bar around the trunk. The Coca-Cola Company would sponsor the Tree on condition that a large advertising sign be erected at the site. Momen dismissed all these proposals as crass commercialism.

Opinions about the work varied, from critics who saw the Tree as an unfortunate intrusion of desert serenity, to others who heralded the work as a sophisticated piece of environmental art. Some local reports questioned Momen's generosity in embarking on such a costly endeavor and then magnanimously donating it to the people of Utah. Proposals to construct a pullout for motorists at the site were condemned by some for encroaching on Utah's skimpy road finance. However, many applauded Momen for his innovation, his generous spirit, and his artistic sensibilities. While some critics, such as Katherine Metcalf, proclaim the work to be the product of a sterile Bauhaus aesthetic, reflecting a "pre-ecological, monument-making consciousness that is very far from the 'site-determined' works that are created in the western desert by younger artists such as Nancy Holt, James Turrell, and the late Robert Smithson," others saw almost the opposite point of view. Namely that the Tree was in fact site-specific, that it was the product of a particular reading of the stark landscape, and that it engaged the landscape in a unique and elemental discourse. It could be said that the Tree was in fact prompted by its maker's particular experience of this unique and very specific location, although his artistic sensibility may have been focussed on an alternative reading of the environment. There is no doubt that Momen was a product of the abstract constructivist movement exemplified by the work of Russian artists such as Naum Gabo, Antoine Pevsner, and Kashmir Malevich. Whether or not the aesthetic of pure form is relevant or not at the beginning of the 21st century is debatable. The fact that this aesthetic survives in Momen's work is not an anachronism as much as it bears witness to the tenacity with which this artist embraced its tenets of significant form. Moreover, the fact that the Tree did not meet everyone's expectations does not necessarily detract from its function as a significant public sculpture in purely ethnographic terms. Adopting a less harsh critique Carol Nixon, the Director of the Utah Arts Council noted: "The artist's job is not to create something that will satisfy everyone—it's to 'create dialogue' and present new ways of viewing the world."

Utah environmentalists did not seem particularly concerned about the Tree. Utah Wilderness Association coordinator Dick Carter proclaimed: "With all the important environmental issues facing the state, I'm stunned that anyone is making a fuss about it." Environmental activist Alex Kelner said that he was "not offended" by the sculpture, "I'm much more offended by high rises in the canyons—they're much more permanent." Kelner expected vandals to mar the surface and thought that it was just a matter of time before the marshy environment eventually claimed the Tree. Momen was unmoved by his environmental critics: "What about Mount Rushmore?" he countered at the time.

An avid supporter of the project, Scott L. Beesley wrote to the editor of the Deseret News that he thought that Momen should be made "an honorary prophet of his adopted state of Utah." Springville Art Museum Director Vern Swanson appreciated Momen's work as "architectonic" and thought that it was Momen's intention to "enlarge the dot on the Utah map of art history that Smithson had created." Other more utilitarian views were expressed by those who saw no value in the expenditure of money on anything that did not result in materialistic advantage to the poor and needy. Olle Granath, director of the Museum of Modern Art in Stockholm, stated: "There is a kind of poetic craziness in the project which ought to get encouragement." As far as he knew there was no Swedish artist who had made such a large international creation. Stig Johansson, a prominent Swedish art critic and writer, saw the Tree as "a sparkling mosaic giving life to something generally the most sterile that exists." On the other hand Janet Koplos, writing in the Asahi Evening News condemned the Tree as something "drained of life." She saw it as something "petrified," consisting of "spheres attached to a column without the least intimation of growth, movement or even grace." Significantly, Koplos had never seen the Tree in the desert and her response was based upon a photograph of an early painting that Momen had executed in 1974.

Momen always reserved judgment on his creation, allowing people to form their own opinions. He knew that people would have their own interpretations and it was for this reason that he had at an early stage contemplated naming the piece "Metaphor." He proclaimed that the tree was the most elemental symbol of life and that in this work he brought together the disparate elements of space, nature, myth and technology. He acknowledged that we live in a world in which technology has taken the helm, and the Tree represents the tension that exists between the natural world and the world of technology. On other levels the Tree also represents the confrontation between life and death, hope and despair. Momen did not want to load his icon with too much literal meaning. In the end he proclaimed: "I don't want to be a messenger. I'm just an artist."

Overleaf: *Momen decided to position some of the quadrant molds that were used to cast the spheres, near the base of the Tree, like giant egg shells that had served their purpose.*

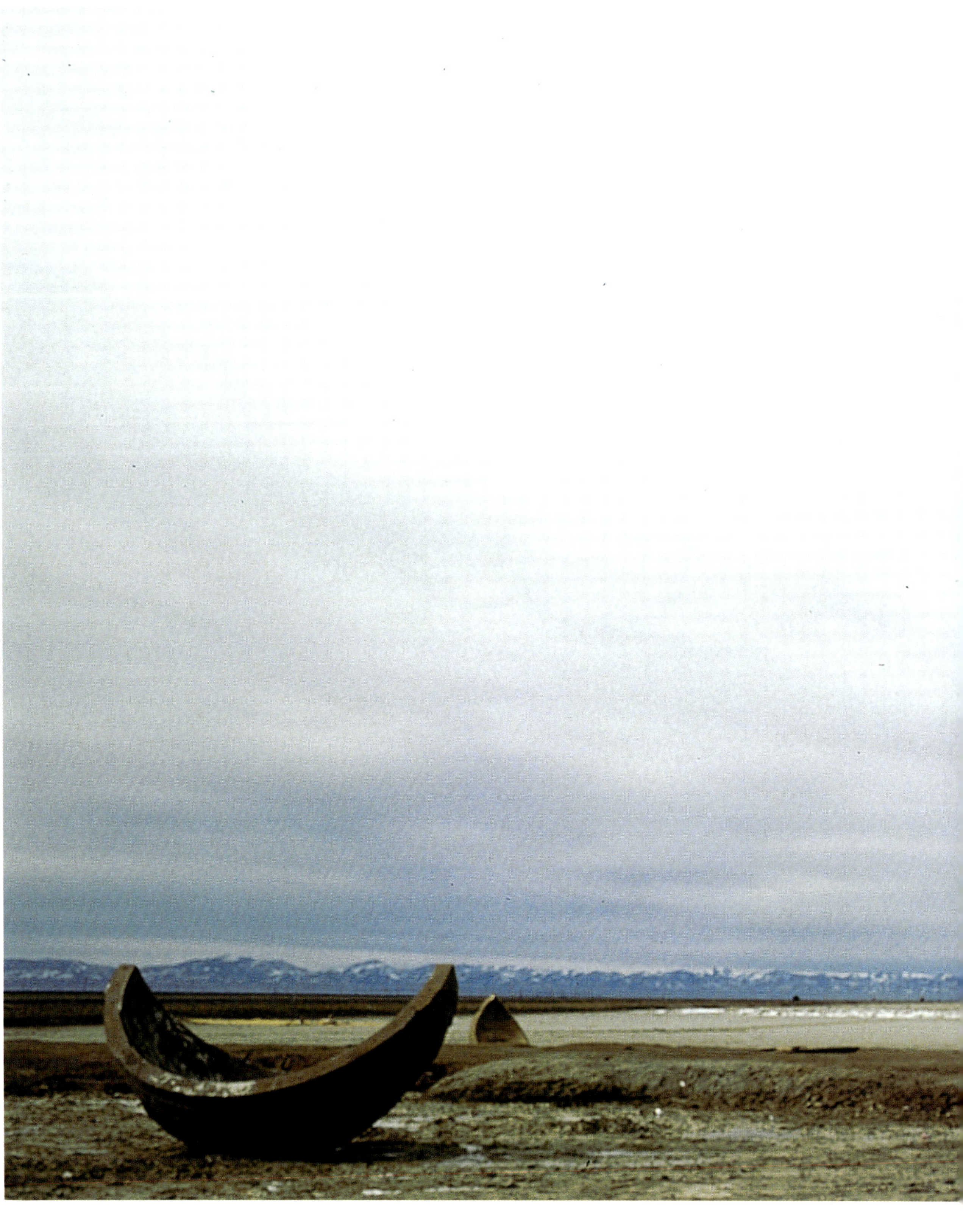

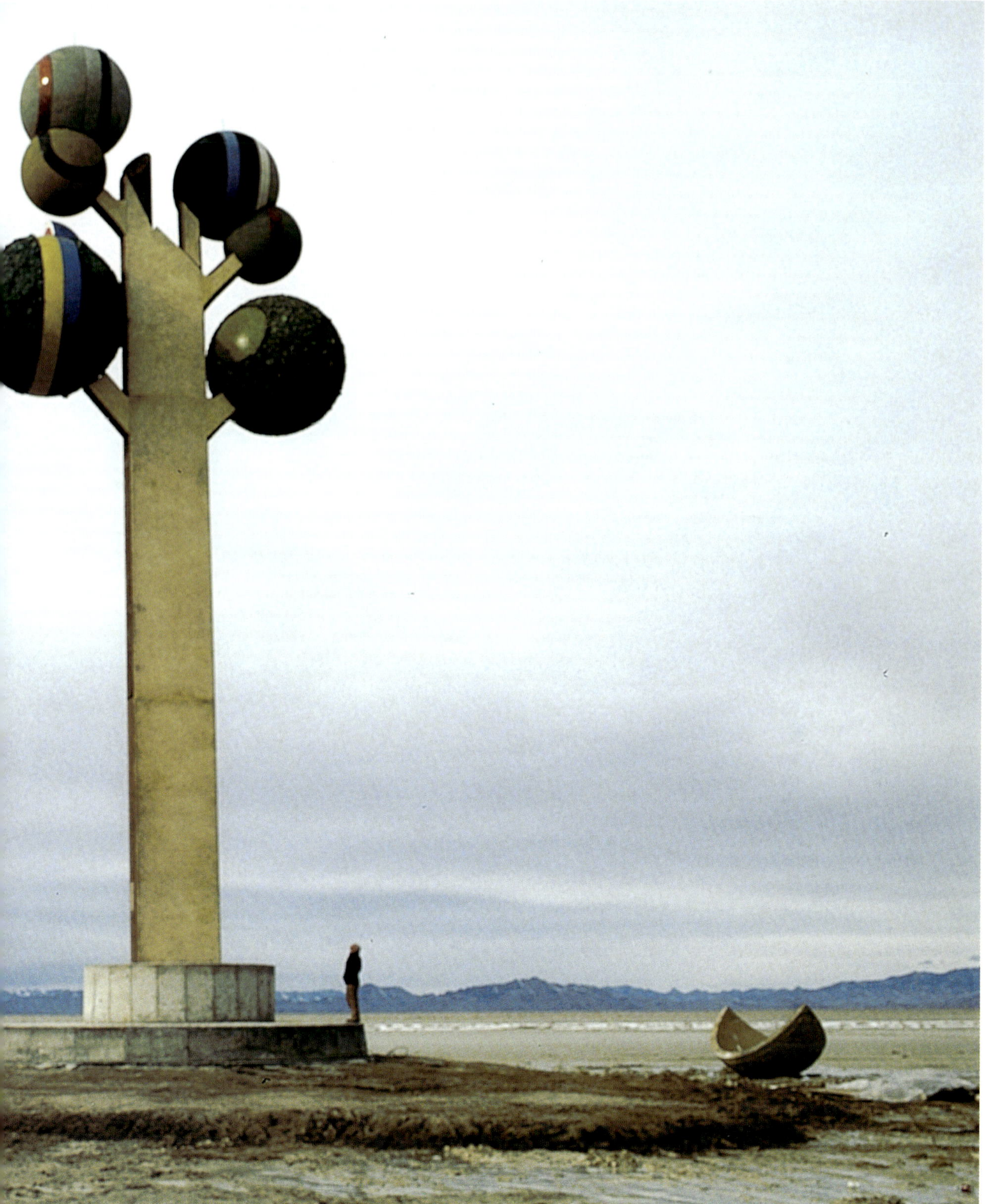

Chapter eight

CONSTRUCTIVIST ANTECEDENTS

Karl Momen's formative years as an artist were affected by the development of some of the most influential movements that helped to shape the direction of twentieth-century art in the west. The underlying precepts and aesthetic principles that permeate both his painting and sculpture can be traced to ideas about the nature of art and the role of the artist that came to the fore in central Europe during the second decade of the twentieth century. Momen lived at a time and in a geographical region that allowed a rich legacy of artistic practice and ideologies. The Russian Revolution of 1917 had precipitated a profound political and social transformation which in turn had given rise to an energetic artistic avant-garde. Vladimir Tatlin, El Lissitzky, Aleksandr Rodchenko, and others seized upon this moment in history to give expression to a utopian aesthetic that they hoped would pervade all aspects of post-revolutionary society. For many the Revolution became the watershed that would unleash the creation of a new social and aesthetic order. Russia had created a zone of influence in northern Persia during the years preceding the Revolution, but Momen's birthplace was shielded from the political grasp of Soviet expansionism by the ascendancy of Reza Khan, a strong local leader who established the Pahlavi dynasty in the early 1920s. The country embarked on a program of modernization and in March 1935, one year after Momen's birth, the country was renamed 'Iran.' In 1941 Reza Khan was forced to give up the throne as a result of his alliance with Germany, to whom he had looked as a neutralizing influence for Russian and British designs on his country. He was later followed by his son Mohammed Reza who became Shah of Iran in 1941. The Shah's dynamic leadership transformed the country into a modern industrial nation until he was overthrown in 1979 by reactionary Muslim forces led by Ayatollah Ruhollah Khomeini. It was during the period of progressive expansion and economic growth, prior to the Khomeini re-

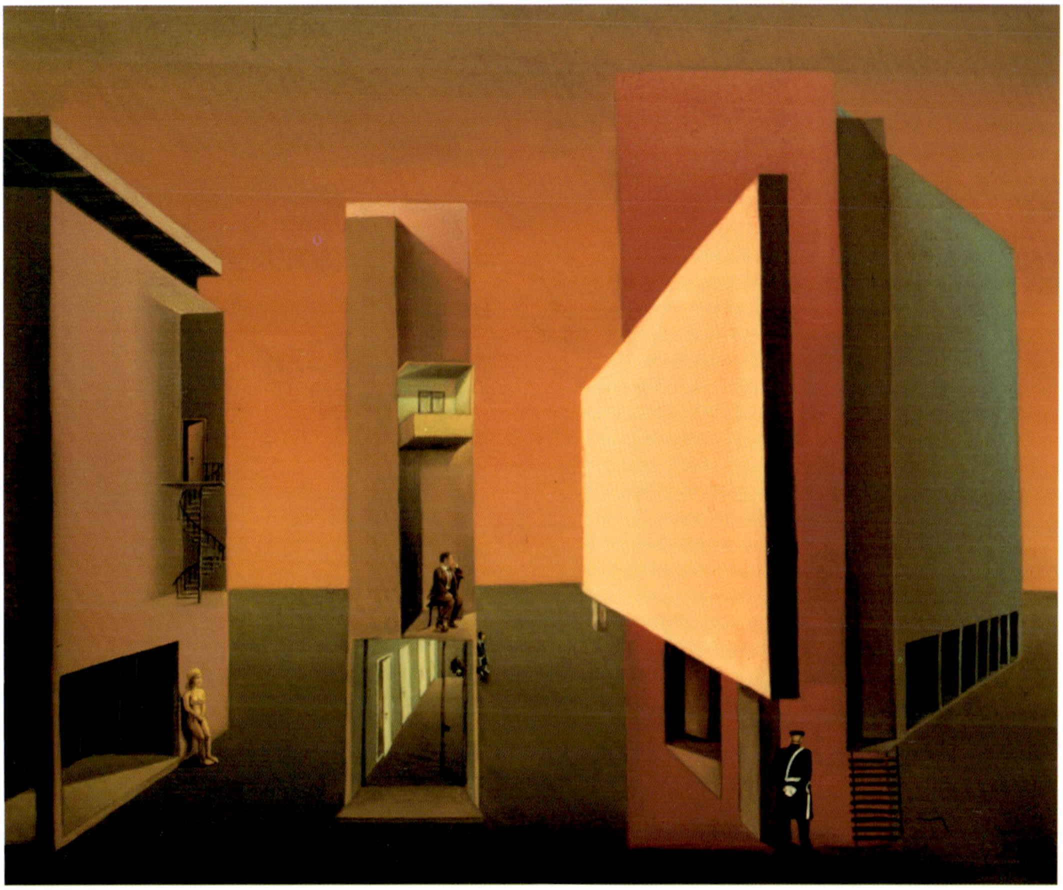

Dawn at Centre of the City, 1970
Oil on canvas

gime, that Momen was raised as the son of a Persian carpet and Oriental ornament designer in northern Iran.

Momen was never partisan to the political ideology of Soviet collectivism and had left his homeland in 1957 to study architecture in Germany, long before the ascendancy of the Ayatollah. He had, however, been exposed at an early age to the influential forms created by the new art movements that were established in the years after the Russian Revolution. It should be remembered that Urie Popow, one of his childhood art teachers, had been an influential member of the Russian avant-garde during his day, and was instrumental in introducing the young Momen to the work of Tatlin, Malevich, and El Lissitzky, in particular.

The influence of the Russian avant-garde on western notions about art and art making has long been underestimated. Only since the fall of the Soviet Union, and the relaxation of restrictions, have publications by Russian and Western scholars produced a clearer picture of the breadth of these progressive movements' origins, aspirations, and pervasive ideologies. Within the Soviet Union a conservative counter-movement had grown during the Stalinist period, that demanded an art of realism and ideological reinforcement. These pressures culminated in the 1932 decree that led to the abolition of independent artists' associations and established Soviet Socialist Realism as the official art of the Soviet people. The voice of the avante-garde was silenced and a full picture of this period has yet to emerge. The publication of Soviet research in England during the 1980s and 90s by Anatoli Strigalev, Selim O. Khan-Magomedov, Anatole Senkevitch, Jaroslav Andel, and other leading Russian scholars, has contributed much to our understanding of the seminal ideas that permeated the short-lived avant-garde movement in East Europe at the beginning of the 20th century. English researchers Christina Lodder at the University of St. Andrews, Scotland, and Stephen Bann at the University of Kent, England, have also done significant work in developing western scholarship in this field.

The definitive characteristics of Momen's painting and sculpture can be traced back to new forms, conventions, and ways of looking at art that were established by avant-garde artists working in the Futurist, Suprematist, Constructivist, and architectural Rationalist movements in the first few decades of the twentieth century. The ideas underpinning the Russian Constructivist movement are of particular interest in an analysis of Momen's production-based aesthctic. It is perhaps no mere coincidence that the seminal work of the Constructivist movement was also a tower. The model for Vladimir Tatlin's tower *Monument to the Third International* was unveiled to the Moscow public for the first time in late 1920. It was intended to celebrate the third anniversary of the Revolution and was received with great acclaim. Consisting of four glazed geometric volumes suspended within a spiraling open structure of steel, it was designed to exploit the modern potentials of the new building materials unified in a dynamic construction. Tatlin stated that it was the Constructivists' intention to "unite purely artistic forms with utilitarian intentions."[1] The idea and image of the tower was synonymous with the ideals of the new Soviet state. It soon served as the symbolic touchstone of the avant-garde, who were the aspirations of the new leaders and were reflected in the upward spiral of the structure. The workman-like construction of the piece represented their hopes for a society based on a foundation of industrial technology, stripped bare of the decorative and ornamental trappings of the so-called decadent bourgeois art it was replacing.

Tatlin proclaimed that it was his avowed intent to take "art into life" and to challenge utilitarian design by integrating the newest ideas in art with advances in industrial technology. Thereby it was hoped that socially useful art would be made that would enhance everyday life. Architecture was held to be the ultimate socially useful object of the new art. This attitude gave rise to the messianic concept of the architect as the builder of the new society and its new way of life. It is not surprising that many of the artists of this era turned to architecture as their career of choice—a decision echoed by

Momen three decades later. Although Momen was distanced from the socialist agenda of the Constructivists, their principles permeated the art schools of Europe and forever changed the direction of modern sculpture. Constructive practitioners Naum Gabo and Antoine Pevsner moved to the West and brought their ideas with them; some went to Germany's industrial design oriented Bauhaus, ensuring the spread of constructivist ideas through Europe and later the United States. Momen had stated on several occasions that he had been influenced by the work of Oskar Schlemmer, one of the founders of the Bauhaus. Although quite different in appearance and intention, the underlying attitudes adopted by Tatlin and Momen with regard to such issues as significant form, non-objectivity, and the highly technological use of materials, have a remarkable degree of congruence in these two artists work.

Tatlin became one of the leaders of the avant-garde, along with his friend and sometime rival, Malevich the father of the Suprematist movement. During the early years of his career, Tatlin also shared a studio with Alexsandre Vesnin and Lyubov' Popova who were destined to become leaders of the new Constructivism in the theater and in architecture. The origins of Constructivism can be traced to Tatlin's earlier "reliefs" and "counter-reliefs" executed during 1913 and 1914. Tatlin had paid a visit to Pablo Picasso's studio in Paris in 1913 and it was there that he saw Picasso's three-dimensional "Guitar" executed in sheet metal and wire the previous year. He returned home to Moscow and began working with metal, wire, and wood to make some of the first total abstractions in the history of modern sculpture. These works were three dimensional, abstract, and represented a synthesis of painting and sculpture. They also took into

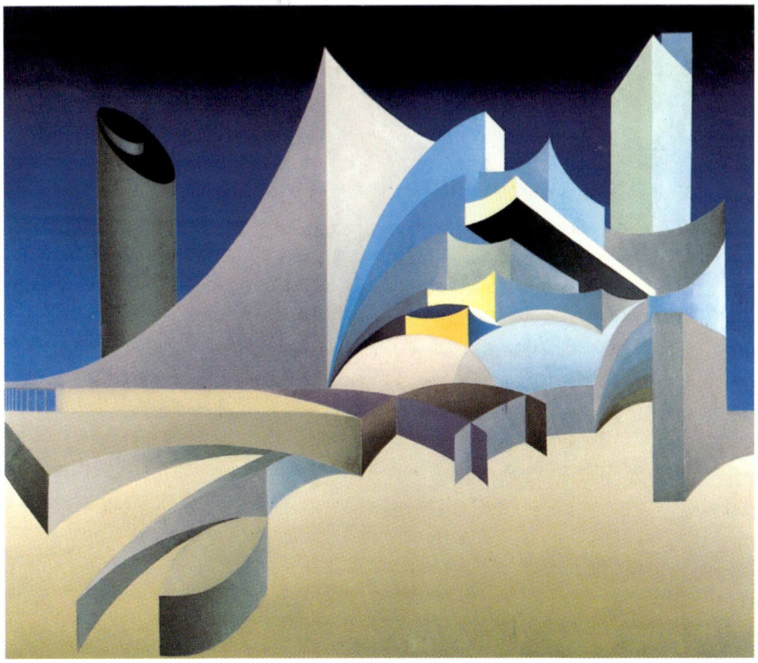

Shangri-La, 1974
Oil on canvas

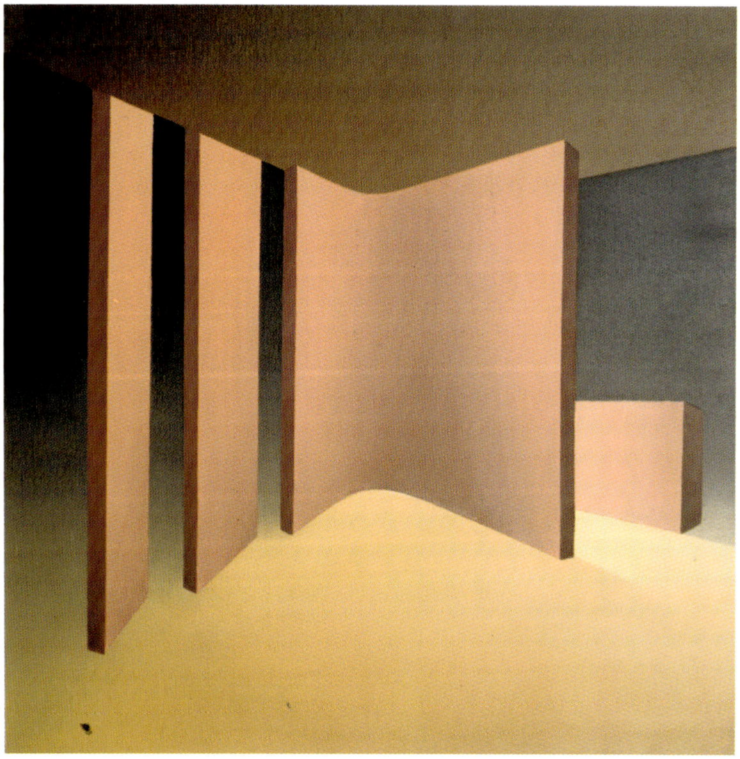

No Exit, 1979
Oil on canvas

account the negative space occupied by the piece, in addition to the mass of the sculptural medium. Soon such works were assembled from traditionally "non-art" materials including metal, wood, glass, plaster, and cardboard, as well as manufactured or "ready-made" objects such as wallpaper or embossed foil. Above all, Tatlin's "reliefs" emphasized the manipulation of real objects in real space—a notion of singular importance to the Constructivists who desired to work in the materials of the new industrial technologies. The actual properties of the materials, their color, surface texture, and form were stressed in their abstract constructions. Significantly, reviewers were aware of the theatrical and architectural potential of these structures from the outset. Constructivism, soon moved beyond abstraction and nonobjective painting to visionary projects in the fields of theater, cinema, poster design, clothing design, furniture design, engineering, communal housing, and architecture. By the mid-1920s the work of the Constructivists was celebrated in the major centers of Europe and in major exhibitions within the USSR, capturing the attention of a generation of art students eager to learn new directions from a charismatic and influential avant-garde.

The artistic principles of the Constructivist movement that inform Karl Momen's artistic vision are best indicated through a review of some key elements of Constructivist theory. Although Western commentators have often regarded the

Voyager, 1980
Oil on canvas

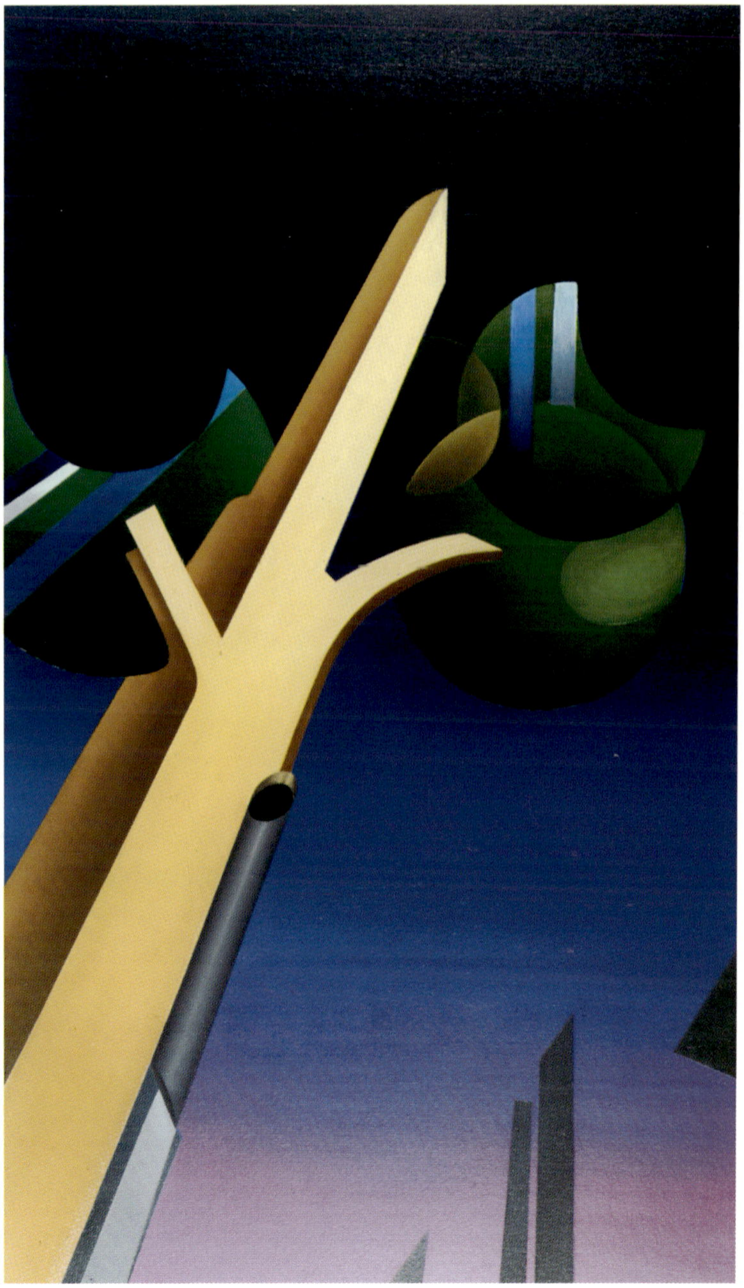

"Realistic Manifesto" of August 5, 1920, as the source text for the creative concept of Constructivism, Selim O. Khan-Magomedov indicates that this text, signed by Naum Gabo and his brother Antoine Pevsner, was but a transitional document. It was in fact intended to demarcate the boundaries between traditional stereotypes and the early stages of Constructivism.[2] The Manifesto therefore gives valuable insight into the context

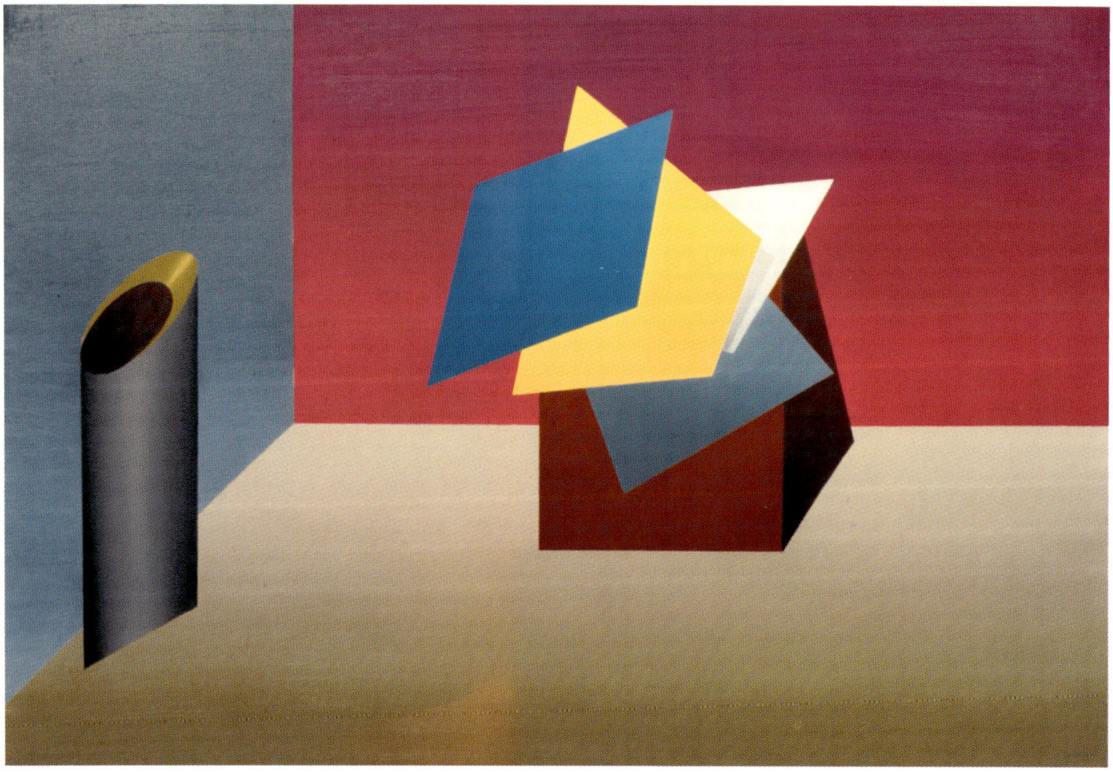

Demolition, 1987
Oil on canvas

within which these revolutionary ideas about art and art-making were first being conceptualized and provides an indication of the potency and radical nature of the new forms advocated by the Manifesto's counter-culture. These ideas would find a constantly renewable life, long after Stalin had all but silenced the voice of the Russian avant-garde. It is also these forms that recur and reverberate in Karl Momen's world of painting and sculpture, notwithstanding the fact that such forms had become decontextualized and remote from their original socio-political roots.

The proponents of the Manifesto decried the ephemeral nature of the art of their day with its many indecisive movements and stylistic quirks. The Manifesto states: "In spite of the demand of the renascent spirit of our time, Art is still nourished by impressionism, external appearance, and wanders helplessly back and forth from Naturalism to Symbolism, from Romanticism to Mysticism."[3] Cubism and Futurism were similarly attacked by the Manifesto—Cubism for not having the capacity to rise above its preoccupation with the simplification of the representational technique; and Futurism for its facile attempts to "fix on the canvas a purely optical reflex which has already shown its bankruptcy with the Impressionists."[4] The Manifesto advocated an art of active engagement in real time and space, declaring that "deed is the highest and surest of truths," all else was seen as mere decoration or superficial embellishment:

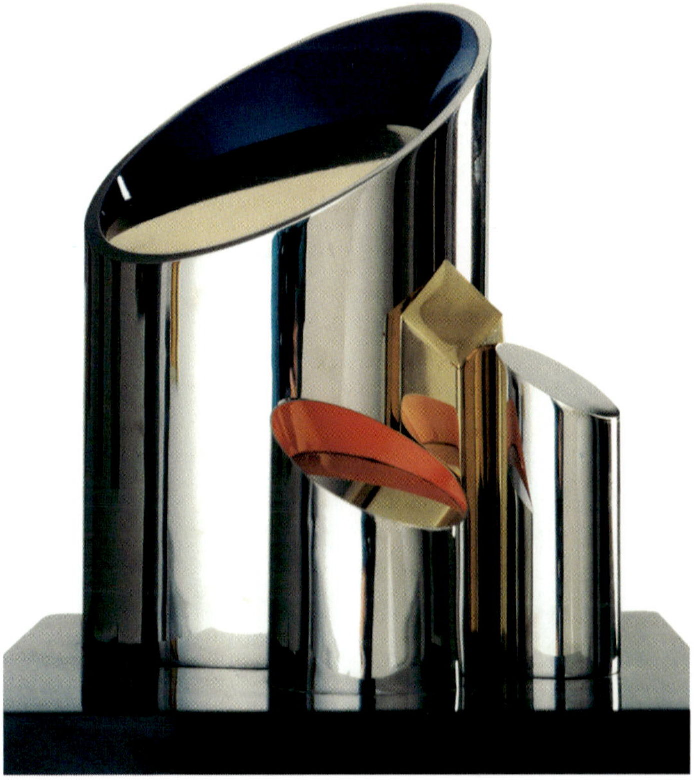

Organ, 1985
Stainless steel

"The realization of our perceptions of the world in the forms of space and time is the only aim of our pictorial and plastic art. In them we do not measure our works with the yardstick of beauty, we do not weigh them with pounds of tenderness and sentiments. The plumb-line in our hand, eyes as precise as a ruler, in a spirit as taught as a compass . . . we construct our work as the universe constructs its own, as the engineer constructs his bridges, as the mathematician his formula of the orbits."[5]

The Manifesto renounced the descriptive quality of line, thereby closing the door to pictorial representation and damning all earlier art to an irrelevant world of decorative visual effects:

"We renounce in a line, its descriptive value; in real life there are no descriptive lines, description is an accidental trace of a man on things, it is not bound up with the essential life and constant structure of the body. Descriptiveness is an element of graphic illustration and decoration. We affirm the line only as a direction of the static forces and their rhythm in objects."[6]

For the Manifesto writers, art should have broad egalitarian relevance. It should be evident everywhere and in all aspects of life:

"In the squares and on the streets we are placing our work convinced that art must not remain a sanctuary for the idle, a consolation for the weary, and a justification for the lazy. Art should attend us everywhere that life flows and acts . . . at the bench, at the table, at work, at rest, at play; on working days and holidays . . . at home and on the road . . . in order that the flame to live should not extinguish in mankind."[7]

Although these precepts appear radical and even severe, they represent the resurgence of new thought that was uncompromising in its attempt to sweep the boards clean so that a new art of relevance and vitality could be established. In doing so, the Constructivists opened the door to powerful real world forms and ways of conceptualizing art that preempted formalism as a movement; shunning sham appearances and facile representation as irrelevant.

The avant-garde artists of the 1920s had moved away from figurative painting and sculpture, having been inspired by the experiments of the Cubists, but later turning their backs on pure abstraction as they developed their own nonobjective forms. In like manner Momen also moved away from the figurative art that he had become so skilled at, and adopted instead an art of abstraction that has its roots in the ideas and forms that arose as a result of the pioneering work of the constructivist artists of this period.

As Constructivism developed, three primary characteristics were identified as the dialectical principles of the program. The first, tectonics (tektonika), referred to the systematic utilization of the latest industrial materials and techniques to produce artistic forms that also reflected the new socialist way of life. This principle was of particular relevance to Constructivist architecture at the time.

The second principle, facture (faktura), was defined by Aleksei Gan, one of the First Working Group of Constructivists as "the deliberate selection and appropriate use of industrial materials whose processed or finished state made them inherently suitable to the requirements of a given design problem."[8] The inherent quality of the material was to be preserved while at the same time directly expressing the nature of its transformation into the finished product. In the Tree of Utah we find Momen turning to the most advanced techniques of pre-cast concrete construction and the use of special materials that are uniquely suited to his goal in realizing the construction of his sculpture. However, no attempt is made to disguise the nature of the materials in the overall construction.

Construction (konstruksiia), is the third principle in the Constructivist dialectic. According to Anatole Senkevitch this principle was the hallmark of the movement and referred not only to the creation of material form through the assembling of viable and appropriate parts to complete the structure, but also organizing and giving intellectual form to the overall concept as well.[9] Each of these Constructivist principles is present to a larger or lesser degree in Karl Momen's work. Momen's Tree of Utah attests to the currency and efficacy of these principles in providing a dialectic that can be traced

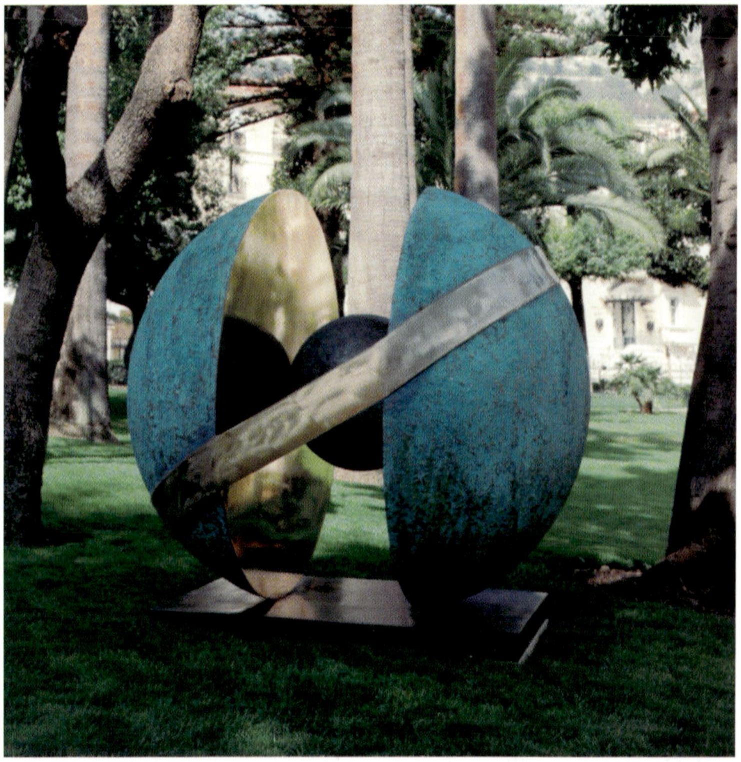

Metropolis, 1990
Cast bronze

back to the ideological and political milieu of central Europe during the first two decades of the twentieth century.

Constructivism gained significant support from its alliance with the contemporaneous Suprematist painting movement. According to Anatolii Strigalev, Suprematism brought about an emancipation in the painting of elementary geometric forms in elementary colors, both chromatic and achromatic, thereby providing a significant precedent for the Constructivists.[10] During the early years of the twentieth century, World War I had forced many expatriate artists to return to Moscow. Among those who returned were Marc Chagall, Wassily Kandinsky, El Lissitzky, and Ivan Puni. These were the halcyon days of the Russian avant-garde and these artists became part of the wave of new experimentation that followed the Russian Revolution. In December 1915 Malevich proposed Suprematism as a name to describe his own paintings at an exhibition entitled *The Last Futurist Exhibition of Pictures: 0-10*, organized by Ivan Puni in Petrograde. Malevich and his colleagues had foreseen the end of the Futurist movement and had united in replacing it with a new movement that would have more relevance to the demands of their time. The term was well received and the majority of avant-garde artists became associated with it. Malevich had supposed that his painting had reached the end point of its advance toward a pure art. He defined Suprematism as "the supre-

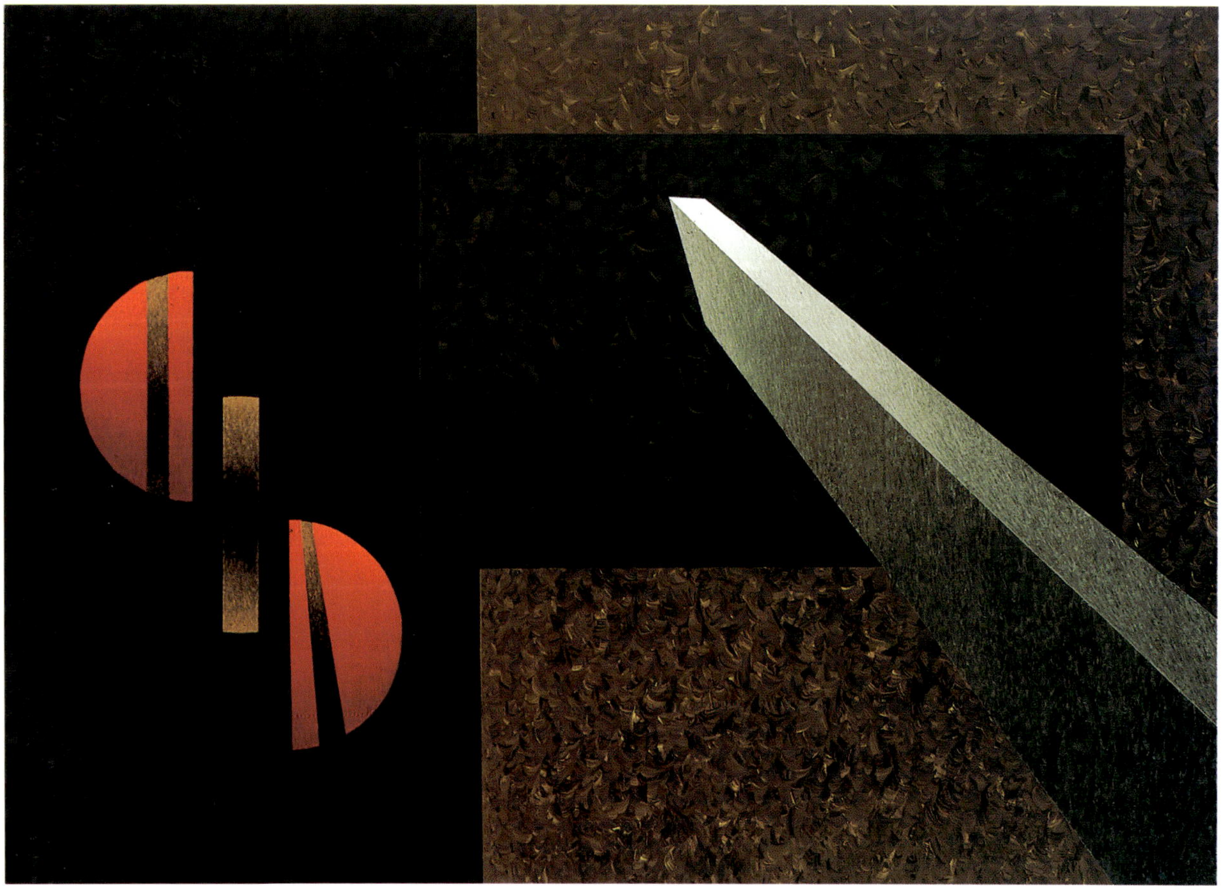

Journey of Titan, 1990
Oil on canvas

macy of pure feeling." He had reduced painting to pure geometric abstraction. Suprematism emerged also as a result of experiments in literature and in avant-garde theater. Malevich's abstract costuming and set designs for *Victory over the Sun* produced in 1913 were examples of such developments. Suprematism united with the central idea of the Constructivists in its attempt to base itself on the achievements of scientific and technical progress, and even make art a stimulus for such progress. Aleksandr Rodchenko exemplified the use of the simplest and "most correct" geometrical forms in his work of 1919 and 1920. He employed solid, even areas of color, using instruments such as the ruler, setsquare, compass, and spray gun. Suprematist ideas spread to the Bauhaus through El Lissitzky and Moholy-Nagy and quickly becoming part of modern art's international venacular.

It should be noted that this group of artists were also teachers who used the new Institute of Artistic Culture (Institut khudozhestvennoi kul'tury, INKhUK) to promulgate their ideas. The Moscow INKhUK operated from 1920 to 1924 and was one of the most important centers in which Constructivist and Suprematist thought and practice developed. The curriculum of the INKhUK was established by a Presidium that was headed by Kandinsky. However, Kandinsky had established a controversial and highly subjective method of art analysis that drew criticism from his peers. Consequently, his concepts were countered with the "objective method" of instruction. The proponents of the new method gathered around Rodchenko who set up within the INKhUK the Objective Analysis Working Group who were to become the teachers of Constructivism when the institution opened in the autumn of 1920. Under the "objective method" of instruction new pedagogic disciplines were established for the foundation course in particular: "Space" (Ladovskii, Krinkii), "Volume" (Lavinskii, Korolev), "Graphics" (Rodchenko), and "Color" (Popova). This format became widespread throughout Europe and provided the model for foundation courses in the arts for many decades to come. In the INKhUK the year of 1921 was designated the year of "construction," and their slogan was "from representation to construction."[11]

The leaders of the First Working Group of Constructivists, Rodchenko, Stepanova, and Gan, held their first meeting on April 28, 1921. The record of this meeting shows the use of the terms "Constructivism" and "Constructivist." These terms arose as a peculiar synthesis of two related concepts that had been adopted from technical design and were being interpreted in a new way by these artists. "Designer" ("konstructor") was the designer of a public spectacle and its artistic organization. "Construction" ("konstruktsia"), was a particular kind of organization of the structure of an art work. Whereas the words: "konstruktsia" and "konstruktor" were loaded with semantic associations, the new terms "konstruktivizm" and "konstruktivist" were free from associations and found ready and easy acceptance. So the concept of Constructionism was born and became part of the mindset of the early twentieth century art world. It was a very powerful and pervasive concept that found reinforcement in the upsurge in the new technologies of the industrializing societies of Europe and in the need for new cites and methods of housing growing urban populations. It is also the essence of thinking, stripped bare of its socio-political agenda, that underpins the theoretical principles of Momen's modernist aesthetic.

In 1962 geometric elements resembling the Tree of Utah first made their appearance in Karl Momen's architectural drawings. As a practicing architect at the time, he had been commissioned to design a pathologic institute for the Karolinska Institute in Stockholm, Sweden. Architects often make use of abstracted impressions of shrubs and trees as landscape elements in their renderings of proposed buildings. Momen developed a stylized interpretation of a tree that used a trunk supporting spheres of differing sizes. These spheres would often gently impinged on each other like under-inflated beach balls that flatten at their points of contact. This particular abstraction recurred in Momen's architectural renderings of trees that he produced at his practice in Sweden during the 1960s.

Momen's characteristic tree symbol first made its appearance in some of his major paintings in the early 1970s. *Structural Change* (1972-74) and *Detonation* (1974) both include this now familiar symbol. *Structural Change* was exhibited in various international galleries in 1978 to 1982, including the Striped House Museum in Tokyo in 1978 and the Berlin Cultural Center in 1982. It was shown at the Springville Art Museum in Utah in 1984 and the following year in the Salt Lake Art Center. For Momen the recurring image of the tree in his paintings was a veiled reference to concerns with environmental issues that were prevalent during the 1970s. In Momen's iconography the tree became a symbol that represented the natural order of all living things—an order that was under assault by rampant industrialization and urbanization. The tension between nature and man became the dominant subject of his painting *Structural Change*. Momen also had a desire to express his concern for the dangers of the nuclear arms race at the time. His use of spherical forms in *Detonation* evokes the awesome power of nuclear fission and stands as an injunction to its destructive use.

Momen was always very proud of his Persian heritage. He often alluded to his cultural roots through the use of bright primary colors in his compositions. His palette often reflected the vibrant colors of the dresses and costumes of the ethnic Russian people that he knew in his childhood. These pure colors accorded with the pure colors so often used by the Bauhaus school of design. Pure colors were also the preserve of the wool dyers in his native Masshad where he was familiar with the large pools of dye that were used to color the woolen yarn used in Persian rug weaving. His early exposure to the geometric abstraction of the Constructivists and the Suprematists was further reinforced through working with Uri Popow on mural and interior decoration commissions in Masshad in his youth. Popow would employ the teenage Momen to assist him in applying stencils and stucco moldings in house interiors. The colorful motifs that Popow used were derived from the abstract geometric patterns that he had beheld in the work of the avant-garde painters that he had tried to emulate in his own non-commercial paintings. These forms became deeply imbedded in the young Momen's subconscious mind, resurfacing in later years as strong elements of his abstract sculptural and painting compositions. These early percepts were later reinforced and honed to a high level of sophistication by the years he spent working in the Scandanavian design field as an architect. Art museum director and art historian Vern Swanson identified this singular characteristic as Momen's 'architectonic' sensibility.

The influence that Russian icons had on the formative years of the young Momen can not be underestimated. During his adolescence he was often commissioned to make copies of Russian icons on wooden panels for the local religious community in his hometown. The Gestalt properties inherent in these images left an indelible impression on his young mind. This particular sensibility was reinforced by his Bauhaus-inspired

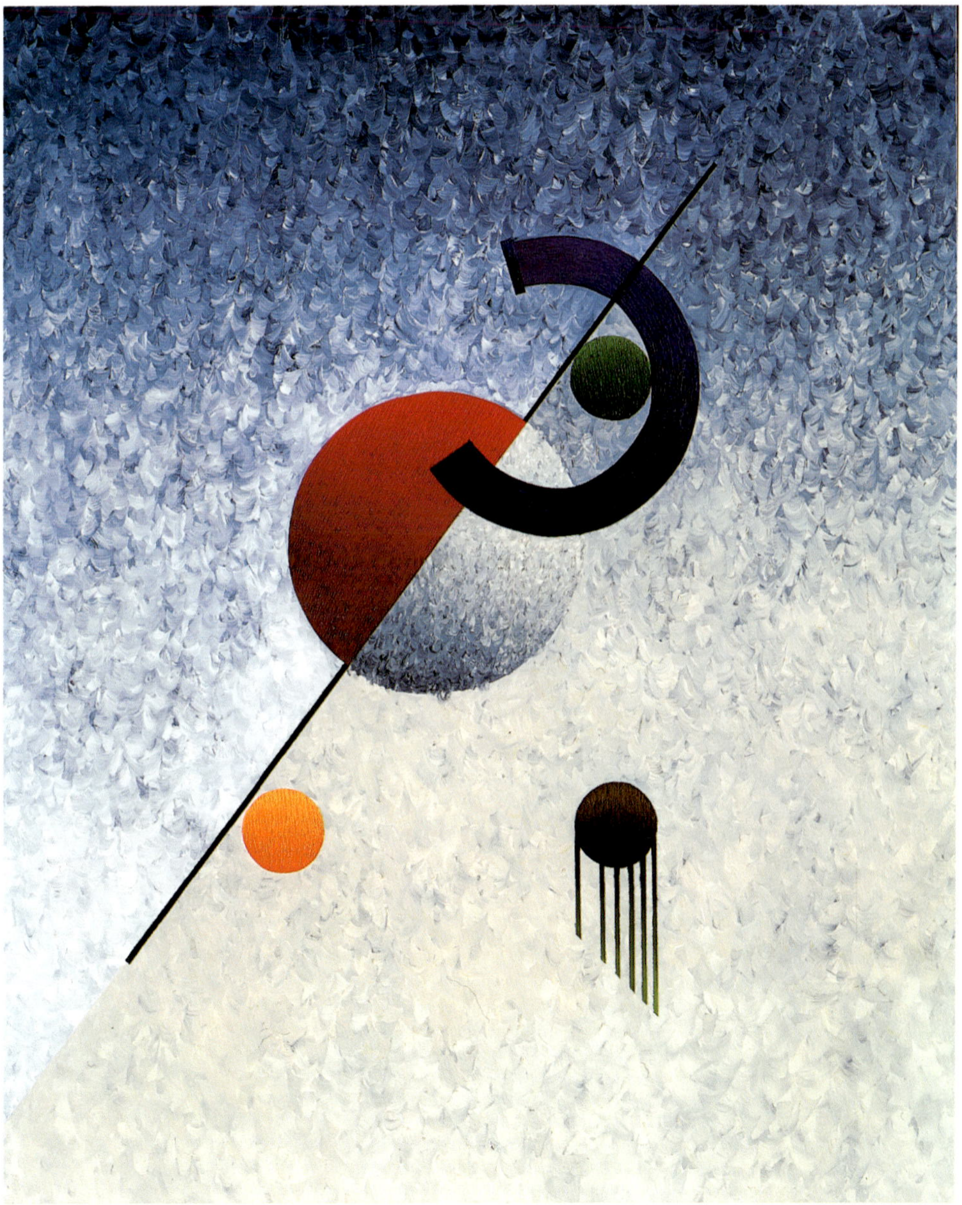

Cosmic Superlative IV, 1993
Oil on canvas

training and was to find expression years later in the predominance of iconic elements and motifs in his painting and sculpture. His intuitive awareness, and striving for, strong figure-ground relationships is no where better expressed than in his construction and siting of the Tree of Utah in the flat, barren desert.

However, it should be remembered that, for Momen the recurring image of the tree was also a veiled reference to concerns with environmental issues that were prevalent during the 1970s. In Momen's iconography the tree became a symbol that represented the natural order of all living things—an order that was under assault by rampant industrialization and urbanization. This tension between nature and man is the subject of his painting *Structural Change*, which also expressed his concern for the dangers of the nuclear arms race at the time. His use of spherical forms in the work *Detonation* evokes the awesome power of nuclear fission and stands as an injunction to its destructive power. In later years Momen was to interpret his Tree as a symbol of preservation and survival that also represented the essential beauty of the American nation.

Art critic Katherine Metcalf interpreted Momen's artistic sensibility as "*a sense of beauty that advocates of purism such as Le Corbusier and Ferdinand Leger found in the smooth, functional forms of a ship, a plane, a teapot. It is a sense of beauty with a strong undercurrent of mysticism in the manner of Wassily Kandinsky who wrote in 1910 that abstraction was the language of the spirit in the bourgeois, materialist society of the twentieth century. Like Kandinsky in the 1920s so Momen in the 1980s combines his love of color, circles, and cosmic space in a personal hymn to the universe; and like Kandinsky, he is very 'romantic' and musical. The inscription on the trunk of the tree is Schiller's Ode to Joy, as sung in the choral climax of Beethovens's Ninth Symphony.*"

In later years Momen was to re-interpret his Tree as a symbol of preservation and survival that stood for the essential beauty of the American nation and even as a metaphor for the dynamic balance and order of the universe.

References.

1. John E. Bowlt, ed., *Russian Art of the Avant-garde: Theory and Criticism 1902-1934*, New York,Viking, 1976, pp. 205-6.

2. Selim O. Khan-Maomedov, "Early Constructivism: From Representation to Construction" in Richard Andrews, ed., *Art Into Life: Russian Constructivism 1914-1932*, New York, Rizzoli International, 1990, p.

3. Naum Gabo, Noton Pevsner, *Realistic Manifesto*, Second State Printing House, August 5, 1920, Moscow.

4.Ibid.

5.Ibid.

6.Ibid.

7.Ibid.

8. Anatole Senkevitch, Jr. "The Sources and Ideals of Constructivism in Soviet Architecture" in Richard Andrews, ed., *Art Into Life: Russian Constructivism 1914-1932*, New York, Rizzoli International, 1990, p.171.

9. Ibid.

10. Anatoli Stragalev, "The Art of the Constructivists: From Exhibition to Exhibition, 1914-1932" in Richard Andrews ed., *Art Into Life: Russian Constructivism, 1914-1932*, New York, Rizzoli International, 1990, p. 26.

11. Ibid. p. 51.

Ownership Passes to the State of Utah

On September 25, 1996, the Tree of Utah was formally, and finally, accepted by the State of Utah at a special ceremony at the State Capitol in Salt Lake City. The new Utah governor, Mike Leavitt, officially accepted the Tree, and the land on which it stands, from Karl Momen on behalf of the people of Utah. Ownership of the Tree now rests with the State and its agencies.

This simple ceremony marked the culmination and full realization of Momen's vision in the desert and brought finality to the project in all its many Constructivist dimensions. However, Momen did not relinquish interest in the ongoing care and preservation of his creation. He has actively promoted the Tree and continues to express his concern for the care and maintenance of the sculpture now that it is in the care of the State. It is the State of Utah's prerogative to ensure that the sculpture is properly protected and maintained, and that it becomes accessible to the people of Utah and the many visitors to this region who pass by it daily on Interstate 80.

Governor & Mrs. Michael O. Leavitt,
the Utah Arts Council,
and the Utah State Division of Facilities
and Construction Management
invite you to attend
a ceremony marking the donation
on it's tenth anniversary,
of *Tree of Utah* by Karl Momen
to the State of Utah.

Governor's Office
Utah State Division of Facilities and Construction Management
Utah Arts Council

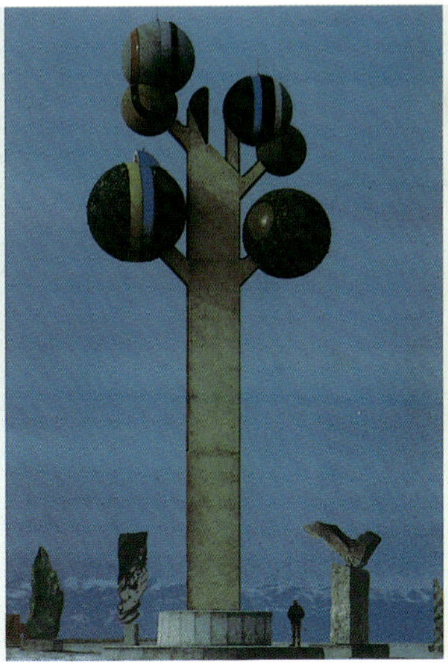

Wednesday,
September 25, 1996,
Governor's Board Room
Utah State Capitol
1:45 p.m.

Tree of Utah will become
part of the Utah State DFCM Collection
of Fine Art as the centerpiece
of a future international
sculpture park.

For more information
contact the Utah Arts Council at
801- 533 - 5895

Program for the dedication ceremony of September 25, 1996 at the State Capitol in Salt Lake City.

Karl Momen

Karl Momen is a Swedish artist, born in Mashad, Iran in 1934. He was educated in art and architecture in Germany from 1957 to 1962 and has resided in Stockholm as a Swedish national since 1962.

He has exhibited widely at various museums, art centers, and art biennials. His paintings and sculptures are represented in numerous public and private collections in Europe, the United States, and Japan. Karl Momen's major work is The Tree of Utah, which was completed in 1986, and stands 87 feet high in the Great Western Desert, in Utah

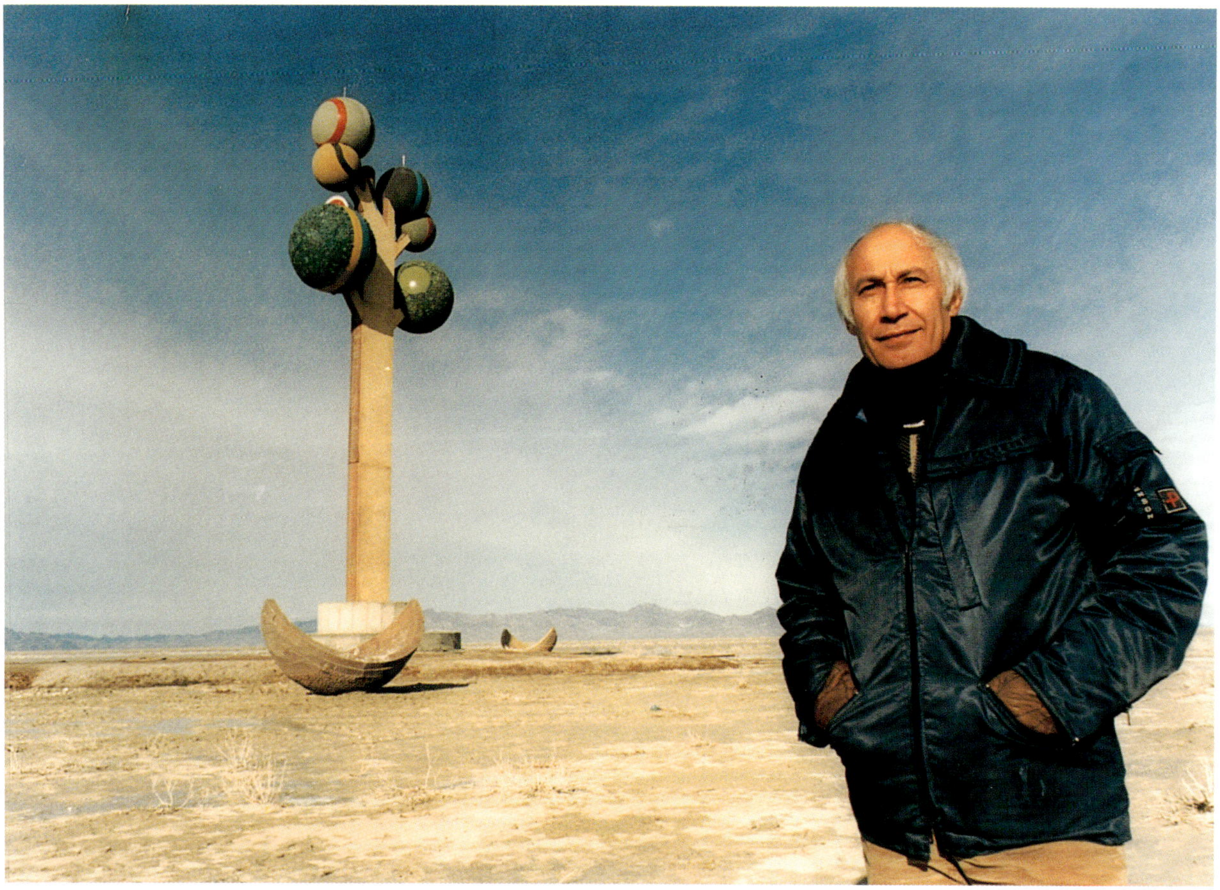

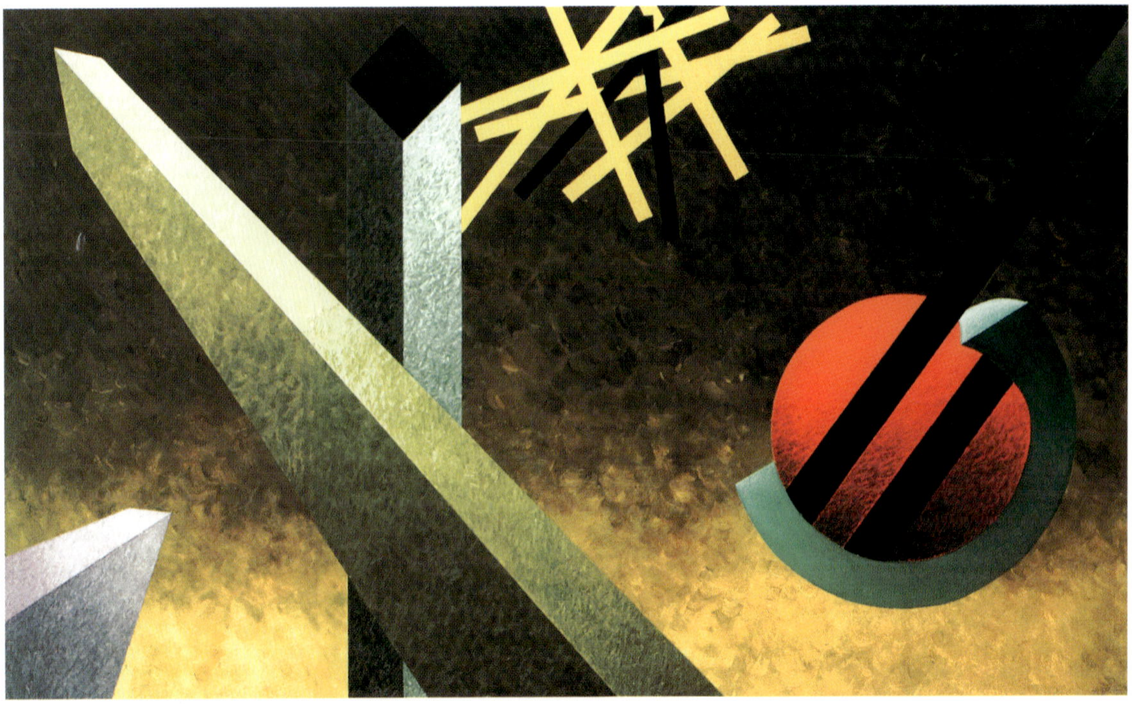

MAJOR EXHIBITIONS

Collective Exhibitions:	
Metropolitan Museum & Art Center, Miami	1977
Museum of Modern Art/Moderna Museet, Stockholm	1982
Monte Carlo Biennal, Monte Carlo	1989
Monte Carlo Biennal, Monte Carlo	1991
Monte Carlo Biennal, Monte Carlo	1993
Utah Museum of Fine Art, Salt Lake City	1996
Utah Museum of Fine Art, Salt Lake City	1998
Solo Exhibitions:	
Haus am Lützowplatz, Cultural Centre, Berlin	1979
Salt Lake Art Centre, Salt Lake City	1985
Springville Art Museum, Utah	1985
Striped House Museum, Tokyo	1985
Haus am Lützowplatz, Cultural Centre, Berlin	1989
Brigham Young University Museum of Art, Provo, Utah	1996

Captive Giant,
1987
Oil on canvas

HERMAN DU TOIT

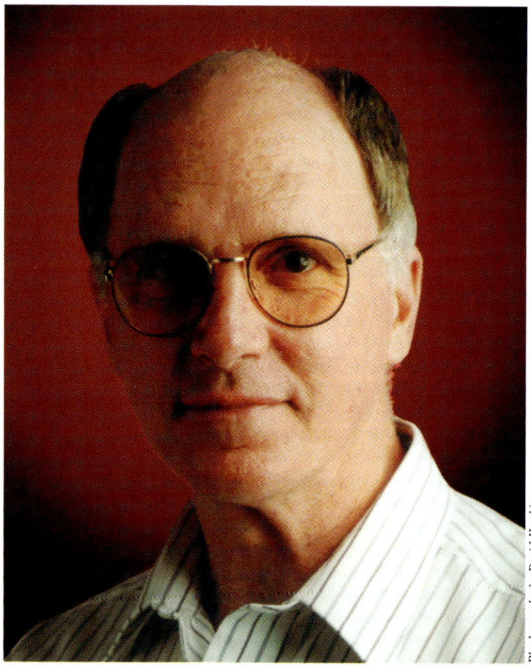

Photography by David Hawkinson

Herman Du Toit is head of audience education and development at the Brigham Young University Museum of Art in Provo, Utah. He has enjoyed an extensive career as an art educator, curator, critic, and writer, both locally and abroad. He is a previous Director of the Durban Art School, and was head of the art education program at the University of Natal, in Durban, South Africa. His special interest in sculpture resulted in his curatorship of exhibitions that have featured the work of some of the most celebrated public sculptors in the United States.

An alumnus of Natal University in South Africa in the fields of art history, sculpture, and sociology of education, Herman Du Toit received his Ph.D. degree from Brigham Young University. He was awarded a J. Paul Getty Doctoral Fellowship in 1996 for his research of educational and interpretive practices at some of America's leading art museums. He and his wife Sandy have four children and reside in Provo, Utah.

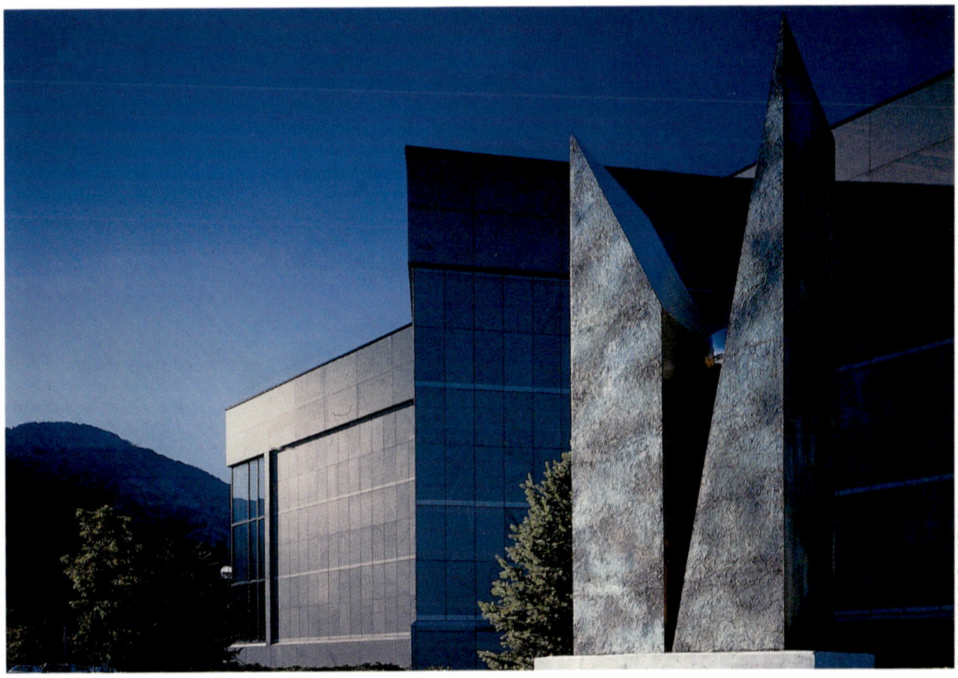

Photography by David Hawkinson

Karl Momen's *Temple of Mercury* was acquired by the Brigham Young University Museum of Art in Provo, Utah in 1995. The bronze sculpture is displayed prominently against the granite façade of the 100,000 square foot, state-of-the-art facility. Brigham Young University is the largest privately owned university in the United States.

INDEX

Numbers in bold refer to illustrations.